Get a Teaching Job NOW

A Step-by-Step Guide

Mary C. Clement

ROWMAN & LITTLEFIELD EDUCATION
A division of
ROWMAN & LITTLEFIELD PUBLISHERS, INC.
Lanham • New York • Toronto • Plymouth, UK

Published by Rowman & Littlefield Education
A division of Rowman & Littlefield Publishers, Inc.
A wholly owned subsidiary of The Rowman & Littlefield Publishing Group, Inc.
4501 Forbes Boulevard, Suite 200, Lanham, Maryland 20706
www.rowman.com

10 Thornbury Road, Plymouth PL6 7PP, United Kingdom

British Library Cataloguing in Publication Information Available

Library of Congress Cataloging-in-Publication Data

Clement, Mary C.
Get a teaching job now : a step-by-step guide / Mary C. Clement.
pages cm
Includes bibliographical references and index.
ISBN 978-1-4758-0335-8 (cloth : alk. paper) — ISBN 978-1-4758-0336-5 (pbk. : alk. paper) —
ISBN 978-1-4758-0337-2 (electronic)
United States. 2. Teaching—Vocational guidance—United States. 3. Job hunting—United States. I.
Title.
LB1780.C475 2013
371.102023—dc23
2012051244

♾™ The paper used in this publication meets the minimum requirements of American
National Standard for Information Sciences Permanence of Paper for Printed Library
Materials, ANSI/NISO Z39.48-1992.

Printed in the United States of America

This book is dedicated to the directors of career centers who have helped the author throughout her career. Special thanks to Mr. Warren Kistner, who shared about behavior-based interviewing.

Contents

Preface

The Science of Getting a Teaching Job

Every fall I get a new group of student teachers and career changers in my college classes. They all want jobs and they all want them NOW. Most have heard the rumors about how challenging the teacher job market is. Many are seeking teaching jobs because their previous job ended with the downturn in the economy. I provide good news: there ARE teaching jobs. I explain how to locate job openings, apply for the jobs available, and how to win interviews to get the job. This book is everything I teach my own student teachers, and they do get jobs.

My students are surprised to learn that they must actively search for a teaching job and should be willing to move to find one. They don't always know that it is much easier to find a job in middle and high schools than in elementary schools. Teachers who can teach math, science, and special education are actually in demand. My student teachers in Spanish never have difficulty finding jobs, and the first elementary majors to get job offers are the ones who have additional coursework in English as a Second Language (ESL), Spanish, special education, reading, math, or science. While there are teaching jobs, the market is competitive and specialized.

When it comes to paperwork, I always have a few student teachers who write their resume the night before their first job fair. Those resumes don't help much, as a good resume has been reviewed and edited by multiple people over time. Just going to a job fair doesn't help either, unless the candidate has prepared a great one-minute sales speech that summarizes why they should be hired and has a user-friendly portfolio to demonstrate to an employer.

In addition to preparing my students with answers to the most commonly asked interview questions, I share the crazy and illegal questions with them. I say, "What will you say if asked one of these questions?"

Candidates who get interviews must be polished, prepared, and positive to get a second interview, and eventually, a job. They must know how to share their experience and expertise in response to behavior-based questions. If they are interviewed by an unskilled interviewer, they must know how to answer bad questions and still provide good answers.

Many of my students share the advice that they have heard about getting a teaching job, and I discuss that advice with them. Often what they have heard is outdated or just plain wrong. One student shared that she was told to wear a bright, colorful dress to job fairs so that she would stand out. She wore a dress that was appropriate for a lawn party and did not get a single short interview at a job fair.

Another student said that "everyone" says that the best way to get a teaching job is to walk into the principal's office and demand to turn in your resume directly to him/her. Later, she actually got banned from a district for this assertive behavior and wasn't even allowed to apply for a substitute job there. Bad advice, indeed.

I have been researching the hiring of new teachers for over twenty years, and I still occasionally get a surprise. Just recently I told a group of seniors in college that they needed a career suit for upcoming interviews. One replied, "What do you mean when you say career suit, and where would I get one?" When I shared an online teacher recruitment site with a class they could see which jobs were available. One student moaned, "I don't see any Kindergarten or first grade openings, and that's all I want to teach."

I forget that every year the new group of job seekers is asking questions because they don't have the information. That's why I have written this book. It's everything about getting a teaching job and it's in one place. You don't have to sort through dozens of online web sites or rely on word-of-mouth advice. There is a science to getting a teaching job now, in today's tough job market.

Many successful job candidates remark that "getting a job turned out to be a job in and of itself." They report that they spent time every week for almost a year getting prepared and searching. The result was a choice of jobs.

My best advice on getting a teaching job is to start your search about a year before you finish your teacher certification/licensure. Read widely on the subject of getting a job, have your cover letters and resume reviewed by multiple people, and know a lot about the districts where you apply. Become an expert at job searching and you can get a job. In other words, just as you will tell your future students, do your homework. This book is a pleasant and very productive way to do your homework.

Introduction

Are you an undergraduate student in a teacher education program getting ready to graduate? Did you teach a few years and then stop-out to start your family? Are you a college graduate looking for a more stable, family-friendly job that allows you more time to raise your children? Does making $35,000 to $75,000 a year appeal to you, with at least two months off in the summer (www.teacherportal.com/teacher-salaries-by-state)? How about retirement in your fifties, not late sixties? Does the chance to run a school, make a six-figure income, and make a difference in the lives of children sound much better than your current job (www.nassp.org/jobs/2010-principal-salary-survey)? If you answered yes to any of these questions, then you are a good candidate to enter the teaching profession and to make a career of teaching.

The stability and family-friendliness of teaching, coupled with salaries, benefits, and vacation time, make teaching a very viable career option (Wiseman, Knight, and Cooner, 2005). There will always be children to teach, and teaching offers tenure in most jobs after two to three years of successful work. Teachers have a set routine. Their bosses don't call on Sunday and ask them to fly across the country to fix a problem, and they aren't on call on holidays. The maternity/paternity benefits are better than many jobs, and some teachers choose to take a one-year leave of absence to start families or even stop-out for several years. This is unheard of in most other professions.

What are some commonly held beliefs about teaching that may not be true? First, many college students are told that they shouldn't major in teaching because "you won't make any money." Noted educator Harry Wong wrote, "teachers are not downtrodden or poor" (Wong and Wong 2009, 51). New graduates who start teaching jobs may make similar salaries, and sometimes more, than their peers with liberal arts and sciences degrees, and the chances to improve the salary with a master's degree or an administrative position are available (www.nea.org/home/38465.htm).

"You are too smart to be a teacher." Students at the top of their high school graduating class may hear this phrase, but honestly, you have to be smart to be a teacher, as today's students need to be challenged academically.

"Today's kids are so bad that you don't teach, you just try to maintain discipline." While there are challenges in today's schools, the completion of a strong teacher education program that includes coursework in classroom management will help you to run a classroom where learning takes place (Wong and Wong, 2009).

"In this economy, there aren't any jobs." There are jobs, and some teachers can pick where they want to work. The teacher job market is strong for those who want to teach special education, math, and science. (See, for example, American Association for Employment in Education, 2013.) Go to teachers-teachers.com or schoolspring.com and read the posted openings. Elementary teachers who have additional coursework in reading, Spanish, or English as a Second Language (ESL) are employable. There are jobs in private schools and jobs for teachers abroad.

SUBSTITUTE TEACHING

Working as a substitute teacher is a way to decide if you want to be a teacher. It is also a way to work your way into a full-time position if you are a certified teacher. In some states, all that is needed to work as a substitute teacher is an associate or bachelor's degree in any major, free training provided by a school district, and completion of paperwork.

How do you find out about becoming a substitute teacher? Visit the web sites of school districts near you and read their materials. Remember that each district's procedures vary, so you will need to complete applications for all districts where you want to work as a substitute. When there is a surplus of fully certified teachers, they tend to be hired first for substitute positions. Working as a substitute teacher looks great on a resume.

If you have answered the question, "Do I want to be a teacher," then the next question for you is, "How do I get a job?" Searching for a job opening, creating the necessary paperwork, and interviewing for a teaching job is different than a job search in the business world. It does take time and preparation.

QUESTIONS FOR THE READER

1. Write about a teacher who influenced your life and made an impact on your success. (Hint: This might be asked in a job interview, too.)

2. Do you want to be this teacher for others? Why?
3. Write about a teacher who didn't help you to learn. In fact, if you ran the world, this would be a teacher you would fire. Now, write about why you would never treat your students this way.
4. Do an online search for teacher salaries. Start by reading the first ones that pop up on your search.
5. Next, do an online search for teacher salaries in your state.
6. Go to the web site for a specific district near you and read their teacher salary scale. Note the differences for having a master's degree and beyond. What does a teacher with twenty-five years of experience make?

Chapter One

Becoming an Employable Teacher

LICENSURE/CERTIFICATION

Each state in the United States has its own guidelines for the licensure or certification of teachers for public schools. In this book, license and certification are used interchangeably, as both words are used in the teaching profession, and the vocabulary varies from state to state. Earning teacher certification means that you have completed a teacher education program for a certain field, and that you hold that license/certificate for a certain amount of time. (See www.education.uky.edu/AcadServ/content/50-states-certification-requirements or www.teachers-teachers.com for state requirements.)

Teaching fields vary from state to state, and generally include:

- Early childhood: The teaching of three- to four-year-olds, but this license may include birth to Kindergarten or older grades.
- Elementary education: This certification area generally covers Kindergarten through 6th grade, but may be an area that covers preschool through 8th grade.
- Middle grades education: Middle grades may be called junior high in a few areas and may be defined by a state as 6th–8th grades or 5th–8th grades. Some states limit middle grades certification by subject area, such as middle grades math, language arts, science, and social studies. A teacher must then be certified in the area or areas in which he/she will teach at the middle grades level.
- Secondary: Teachers in high schools earn their certification for the specific subject to be taught—math, history, English, French, art, music, and the like.

- Certification in special areas, for P–12 or K–12: In some states, teachers are prepared to teach their subject area to all grades. These subjects are generally health and physical education, music, and art.

Additional Endorsements to a Certification

It is often said that the more you can teach, the more employable you are. Each state sets the guidelines for the amount of coursework needed for an endorsement. The state's web site that lists certification requirements should also list endorsement areas. The coursework may be minimal, or it may be the equivalent of a college minor in the subject. Endorsements can include reading, English as a Second Language (ESL), English for speakers of other languages (ESOL), gifted education, or a second subject area. Some endorsements permit the teacher to work with more grade levels. For example, a certified elementary teacher may earn an endorsement to teach preschool, or a secondary teacher may earn an endorsement to teach middle school in certain subjects.

How do certification areas and endorsements make you more employable?

Schools need to hire people with versatility. If you have certification for elementary education, and another candidate's resume states an endorsement in reading, as well as certification, that candidate will probably get an interview, especially if the school is working to raise reading scores of all children.

KEY job hint: Earn as many endorsements as possible while still in your teacher education program. If you are re-entering teaching after a stop-out, take some classes and add an endorsement. This is especially helpful if you are an elementary teacher, because the competitiveness for elementary positions remains very high.

Can I teach without certification?

The answer to this question is yes, no, and maybe. Private schools can hire teachers who are not certified. However, most private schools strive to prove that their schools are better than public ones, so many private schools require teacher certification or require that the new hire earn that certification within a given time frame. It is very difficult to teach all day and then go to school at night and in the summers to earn teacher certification, which is generally a two-to-three-year program if one starts after a bachelor's degree. Private school salaries vary widely and may be as much as 50 percent less than public school salaries, especially for noncertified teachers.

In today's teacher job market, most employers are bombarded with more applications than ever before. They generally sort the applicants by certification first, and nonlicensed applicants don't even get a consideration.

What if I move or find more jobs available in another state?

Certification is only good in the state where it is earned. Once certified in one state, getting full certification in another state isn't quite as hard. Some states have reciprocal agreements, and the only thing you need to do is to complete paperwork and pay a fee. Other states will evaluate your transcript and prescribe coursework and testing to be completed for certification in their state.

Go to the web for the most recent regulations. Type in "teacher certification" and the name of the state where you want to work, or use a national site like those already mentioned for lists of all the state departments of education. Further, take advantage of your college's teacher education department and career center to find this information.

IDENTIFYING TEACHER JOB MARKET TRENDS EARLY

Imagine the frustration of an elementary education major who nears graduation and realizes that 600 teachers apply for each Kindergarten or first-grade position in the district where she wants to work. However, in this same area, elementary teachers with endorsements in special education have job possibilities. Should this student add the necessary courses, or expand her search, or wait until the economy recovers to get the job she wants? Individuals must make these decisions on their own, but it is important to be realistic about the job market.

Long before you start your job search, read the national, state, and local job sites for teacher positions, talk with your advisers, and keep an open mind. There are jobs in all grade levels in some urban areas, and in some growing suburban areas. If you are searching for a job in one district and that district has little growth of student population, or little teacher turnover, you may be waiting a long time for an opening. Consider large cities, other states, and even international teacher jobs. (Go to www.aaee.org for information about teacher demand by regions of the country.)

Do I need certification for overseas jobs?

The answer is yes, and no. There may be some jobs that do not require teacher certification, but the best, highest-paying jobs abroad often require it, as well as experience and a master's degree. The Internet can help you start an international job search. Consider going to a job fair in the United States that recruits teachers, so that you meet people face-to-face and not just over the Internet. Be cautious in your search for overseas jobs, but the opportunities for professional growth can be tremendous. (See, for example, American Association for Employment in Education, 2013). As a starting point, go to www.uni.edu/placement/overseas. Additional web sites include:

www.ciee.org
www.teachaway.com

WORKSHEET

Reviewing Your Qualifications and the Job Market Needs

1. When I create my resume, I will begin with my areas of certification, which are . . .
2. In my state, my certification means that I can teach . . .
3. To get a teaching license in another state where I may job search, I would need to . . .
4. After visiting a national web site for jobs, like www.teachers-teachers.com, or others, I see jobs listed in the fields of . . .
5. After reading my state's job site, I see jobs listed for teachers of . . .
6. After reading a district's web site, I see jobs listed for . . .

Chapter Two

Starting the Job Search

A Timetable

When do I start a job search? And where? Let's start with a timetable.

At least a year before you want a teaching job:

- Start reading web sites for job seekers. Find one that works for you. Try teachingjobsportal.com, teachers-teacher.com, schoolspring.com, and others you find with a search for "teaching jobs."
- Do a search for your state's teacher job web site; teachingportal.com and other sites can direct you to your state's site.
- Find and bookmark the district web sites that are of most interest to you.
- Find and bookmark at least two web sites of professional organizations. Consider the professional organization for your subject matter, such as the International Reading Association, the Council for Exceptional Children, or the National Council of Teachers of English. Also, find and read the site of a teachers' association such as Kappa Delta Pi or Phi Delta Kappa. Some of these sites list job openings and others have extensive resources for job searching.
- Find the job fairs in your area. Attend one a year before you are actually on the job market for practice. Your college's career center can alert you of campus job fairs. Other fairs will be posted on the district and state web sites that you read.
- Get to know your college career center and the services they provide. Take advantage of workshops that they offer and mock interview opportunities. If counselors are available to review and edit your paperwork, make an

appointment and use this service. Find out if your college offers a credentials file service to teacher education job seekers.

- Make sure that you are on track to complete full teacher certification or that you have updated your past teacher certification if returning to teaching.

HINT: Volunteer to work at your college's career fair before you are actually on the job market. You can help recruiters carry their boxes, serve coffee, or simply answer questions and give directions. Doing this will teach you how the job fair works when you attend as a candidate.

About nine months before you want a job:

- Gather the materials to create the necessary paperwork for job seekers.
- Create a sample cover letter, a resume, and an interview portfolio, and have other people review and edit these documents. Some districts will require you to register with an online company, or the state web site, before you can even apply for a job. Create an account on such a web site, and create the necessary paperwork online as well as on paper.
- Start requesting letters of recommendation from college professors, former employers, and teachers with whom you have worked. The easiest way to build a file of letters of recommendation is to use the credentials file service offered by the career center at some colleges and universities. This way, you ask a person to write one letter and send it to the career center. When you need letters, you work with the career center to have the letters sent to potential employers.

HINT: If you graduated years ago, you can still use the services of your alma mater. Do so. Check the online offerings from the career center and make an appointment to meet with a counselor if you are returning to the workforce.

Four to six months before you want to start teaching:

- Read your bookmarked sites regularly.
- Go to job fairs.
- Update paperwork.
- Keep good files of the districts where you have applied.
- Keep the business cards or contact information of personnel directors that you have met.
- Apply for all the job openings in your field.
- Practice interviewing with other teachers, administrators, or on your campus.

- Be prepared for preliminary interviews by practicing answers to the commonly asked questions. (For more on this, see chapter 8.)
- Have a professional message on your voicemail.
- Clean up your online presence including on Facebook.
- Buy an interview suit.
- Go to interviews!

The last three months before you want to start a job:

- Keep interviewing.
- Keep in touch with college professors, the teachers you have met in student teaching or a previous job, and use these people as your professional network.
- Always write follow-up notes to thank those you meet at fairs and interviews.
- Remember that school districts often hire over the summer. Many districts used to offer contracts to teachers in February and March for fall jobs. Those districts may now wait until June or July to hire.
- Keep your interview clothes in top shape. Be ready to interview on short notice.
- Talk with others who are job searching. Forming a support group is a great idea.
- Remember that job searching is a lot of work. In the past, principals often just hired the student teachers who worked in their buildings. Now, the market is much more competitive. Become a competitor!

Chapter Three

Creating the Teacher Resume

The resume represents your preparation and experience. It has to be succinct yet detailed enough to set you apart. It is "you at a glance," and a glance is all it may get if it doesn't grab the reader's attention immediately. Some general guidelines for creating a resume:

- Read examples of resumes provided in this book. Ask a newly hired teacher for a copy of his/her resume. (Veteran teachers often do not have resume, or have very outdated ones.)
- Use the activities provided to guide the writing of your resume.
- Start early—months before you need the resume at a job fair or to apply for a job. Typing up a resume the night before you use it doesn't allow time for editing by others.
- Write out your ideas on a worksheet then prepare the first draft of your resume. Let at least three other people read that draft. Readers can include a teacher, a college professor, and a counselor in your college career center.
- Be prepared to hear differing opinions. Listen to the opinions, then make your own decisions.
- When your resume is ready, save a copy for online use.
- You may have several versions of your resume, as you may tailor the resume to meet a particular job advertisement.
- Use high-quality paper for the resume, and do not add borders or drawings. Content is important not colorful school buses as decorations.
- Teacher resumes are one and a half to two pages in length.
- Use a highly readable, very clear font. Ten to 12-point is best.

- Do not squeeze a lot of text onto the pages. Less is more. Be succinct. Use spaces and keep the resume clear and readable. (Think about all the administrators who wear bifocals!)

ACTIVITY: CREATING YOUR TEACHING RESUME

Complete Contact Information

Name, mailing address, email address, phone

Considerations: If you are moving soon, put both current and future addresses, with dates.

Professional Profile or Objective or Summary of Qualifications (one to two lines)

Certification/Licensure (if not clearly stated in above)

Education

List most recent first. Include degree, major, and minor. Include your grade point average (GPA) if it is high.

List a two-year institution if a degree was earned, not if you took a few general courses.

List coursework away from a college where you graduated if it adds to your teacher certification or is in field that makes you more employable.

Teaching Experience

List most recent first. Include student teaching and significant field experiences.

Experienced teachers should not list field experiences completed before student teaching.

Other Work Experiences

List most recent first. Emphasize action verbs and skills that transfer to teaching.

Special Skills and Awards OR Service and Leadership

List most recent first. Include professional memberships, education honor society membership, and other college awards. Do not go back to high school unless you are a new graduate and that high school award relates directly to your teaching.

    Example: Co-captain of varsity soccer team, 2008–2009.

    (Applicant wants to teach history and coach soccer team.)

References and/or Credentials Available

Creating the Opening on a Resume

The professional profile on a teaching resume is the first one to two lines at the top. These lines are the "attention grabbers" and may sound like advertising copy of your skills. On a business resume, the top lines are the objective, written to point out why you are the best candidate. These lines may also be called the "summary of qualifications." Spend some time thinking about what really sets you apart from other candidates. Things to consider include:

- Was something unique about your student teaching?
- Do you already have successful teaching experience?
- Have you worked in a school that made notable progress in raising student achievement?
- What was unique about your teacher training? Did you earn a bachelor's degree and then earn teacher certification?
- Do you have extra endorsements that make you employable?
- Do you bring skills from a previous career?
- If your college has an excellent reputation, note your alma mater early in the resume and cover letter.

Examples:

Professional Profile: From my University of Illinois program, including junior year abroad at the University of Barcelona, I bring Spanish fluency and cultural understanding to teaching. Fully certified for teaching Spanish, 7–12, in Illinois, my student teaching experience included all levels of high school language.

    (This candidate showcases a strong university, study abroad, and fluency.)

Professional Profile: A year-long student teaching experience has prepared me for full certification in elementary education, K–5. My ESL endorsement and a field experience in Costa Rica add to my ability to reach all students in the classroom.

(Year-long student teaching makes this candidate stand out, especially with an extra endorsement and a diverse field experience.)

Professional Profile: An intensive student teaching experience in Dover Elementary School honed my skills in literacy. Fully certified in Alaska for P–5, reading endorsement coursework I have completed that helps me to raise literacy rates of all students.

(Dover may be well known in the district where the candidate is applying.)

Professional Profile: Earning teacher certification with my master's degree in middle grades education has fully prepared me to teach math and science in grades 6–8. After nine years in the business world, I can make these subjects come alive to adolescents.

(Business experience is important.)

Professional Profile: Two years of teaching at the award-winning Lincoln School provided me with strategies for all P–5 students. Eight hours of recent coursework in special education, and nine in mathematics, add to my full certification in elementary education, P–5.

(Candidate was at an award-winning school and has updated skills.)

Professional Profile: Student teaching in a professional development school, Rittendale Middle, prepared me for all aspects of teaching language arts and social studies. Fully certified for 5–8, my credentials include an endorsement in reading and six semesters of college Spanish.

(This candidate's resume goes to the top of the pile for a school with many Spanish-speaking students.)

When writing your professional profile, be sure to localize it, when possible. If dozens of applicants are from the same regional state university, you may stand out by having student taught in a specific school known for its academics or its record on test scores. Yes, your professional profile may change depending on the district where you apply. If teachers are needed in an at-risk school, lead with your field experience at one. You need to decide what sets you apart from a hundred other applicants, and what you bring to the job.

Write sample professional profiles now. Share with other people and then choose the one that best showcases your skills.

Certification/Licensure

Your professional profile may list your certification. If it is clear enough from your profile, you may not need a separate line. However, because your certification is so critically important, most people choose to state the certification separately. Include all endorsements in this section, as well. Use the specific language of your state on these resume lines.

Examples:

Certification: Wisconsin Type 10 Teaching Certificate for grades K–6.

Certification: P–12 Alabama Teaching License for the teaching of French; endorsement for the teaching of P–12 ESL.

Certification: Tennessee Teaching Certificate, Type 01, Middle Grades Language Arts and Social Studies.

Education: When listing your education, start with the most recent. Include major, minor, and the teacher preparation program. Some older candidates returning to the job force are hesitant to put the year of graduation. That is your decision, but employers will get your official transcripts eventually and will know your age from the transcripts.

Should you include your grade point average? Yes, if it helps your case. If it is not high, you may leave it off, but that may be a red flag to some reviewers. Always include degree work at any community college. Do not include a college where you only took a few courses that transferred back to your college. Include study abroad, if it is at least a semester. Include a city if the university has many branches, or if it is not clear to a reader where the college is located.

What is the reader looking for in your educational background? Many employers have strong opinions about the teacher education programs at certain universities and sort resumes according to the criteria for those institutions. If teacher certification was not earned in an undergraduate program, then employers want to know how you earned that certification.

It is not necessary to include your high school. However, if you are applying for a job in a district where you went to high school, that information may get you closer to an interview. Some large districts like to hire graduates from their own districts, especially if there are multiple schools and you will be teaching at one other than the one you attended. Why? Some administrators feel that you will serve as a role model if you are working back in the district where you graduated. This may be particularly true for minority candidates.

Examples for a recent graduate:

Education:

BA, Elementary Education, Nevada State University, Springfield, 2011
    GPA 3.64/4.0

Associate's Degree, Child Development, Columbia Community College,
2009
    GPA 3.52/4.0; included classes taken as a high school senior

Education:

BA, History, minor in Secondary Education, University of Pennsylvania,
2010
    GPA 3.2/4; one semester at Oxford University, England

Education:

BA, English, minor in French, with Teacher Education, Bardin College, CT
    GPA 4/4

Examples for a career changer:

Education:

Master of Arts in Teaching, Tennessee State University, 2012
    GPA 3.8/4

Bachelor of Science in Chemistry, Tennessee State University, 2000
    GPA 3.5/4; included a minor in biology

Education:

Teacher Certification Program in Secondary English, Northeastern Illinois
University, 2013
    GPA 3.5/4; included teacher internship program in Teach for Chicago

Bachelor of Arts in English, Raney College, Columbia, MO, 2009
    GPA, 2.87/4; included a minor in theater
    (In this example, the candidate does not have a master's degree but earned
teacher certification in a nondegree program.)

Stop and write your education experience now.

Teaching Experience

List your most recent teaching experience first in this section. If you are a recent graduate, your field experiences and student teaching are your experience. Those returning to teaching should list their former teaching experiences and also include student teaching but not anything before that. Career changers should only list teaching experiences here and leave their work experiences for a later section. In describing your experience, consider action verbs.

What do employers want to see? They want to see experience at the same grade level and/or in the same subject as the advertised position. They want to know that your experience with diverse learners matches the student demographics in their system. They want to know if you have impacted and improved student achievement. Employers want to see versatility and flexibility in your experience.

Should you include private school or vacation Bible school teaching experiences? Yes, teaching experience is teaching experience. Referring to full-time or part-time experience in a private school is more important than vacation Bible school. Some candidates worry that listing that experience reveals their religious preference. If you feel more comfortable leaving out vacation Bible school, then do so. If you taught in a private school and did so full time as a certified teacher, that should not be left out. An employer cannot ask if you are of the religion of the private school. It is illegal to ask a candidate anything about their religious preference in a job interview, even if the resume indicates experience at a religious school.

Example for a new graduate in elementary education:

Experience:

Big River Elementary, Big River, Wyoming, spring semester, 2013

- Student teaching, 3rd grade classroom, 21 students, including five special needs
- Completed three weeks of lead teaching; administered spring reading achievement tests; designed and taught two social studies units; wrote differentiated plans for special needs students

Thompson Primary School, Big River, Wyoming, August 2011–May 2012

- Year-long Junior Practicum Blocks, Kindergarten and first grades
- Cotaught a reading unit; tutored students in math; led afterschool music classes

Trinity School, summer 2012

- Lead teacher for vacation Bible school for eight-year-olds; 17 students
- Taught daily lessons and organized three field trips

For a new graduate in secondary education:

Experience:

Main High School, Springfield, IN, spring semester, 2012

- Student teaching, 9th and 12th grade English
- Lead teacher for two weeks; implemented a study course for the high school graduation test; administered the state's graduation test; co-taught a unit on Shakespeare, prepared students for the state writing contest

Olympia High School, Springfield, IN, fall, 2011

- 50-hour practicum experience, 10th grade English
- Developed and taught two units—poetry and Colonial period literature
- Assisted in the after-school SAT prep class

Keystone High School, Indianapolis, IN, spring 2011

- Two-week urban education practicum, 8th–11th grades
- Observed and assisted teachers with at-risk classes; taught five grammar lessons

Examples for a teacher with experience:

Experience:

Canfield Middle School, Canfield, OH, 2005–2009

- 7th and 8th grade language arts teacher; six classes per day
- Increased 8th grade scores on OCAT by more than 5 percent; 2007, 2008

- Won a $4,000 Ohio Reads grant for 7th grade library
- Sponsored "Think About College" days, 2007–2009

Mountain Middle School, Carson, OH, spring semester, 2005

- Student teacher, 6th and 7th grade language arts
- Planned and led tutoring sessions for OCAT tests
- Taught six novels during one semester; implemented "Write On"

Stop and write your teaching experience now.

Other Work Experiences

Your most recent work experiences are listed first. Recent graduates should include summer jobs and part-time college jobs, emphasizing ones that included working with children. Working as a camp counselor, a swim instructor, or a tutor adds to your resume. Some administrators like to see continued work experience. Working three summers at a bank indicates that your work was so strong that the employer wanted you back every summer. With each work experience, you may add a line or two with action verbs about your work, especially if it involved teaching or leadership.

Those who are re-entering teaching after a stop-out need to list their most recent teaching experiences first, emphasizing accomplishments. Administrators want to know if you were successful in your last job, and success is often measured by test scores and additional duties that served students. List student teaching but not short field experiences, unless they were in a school that the future employer would recognize.

Career changers who are seeking their first teaching job will list previous jobs, with a few lines about their duties. Most employers are looking for stability in the position and also for skills that transfer to teaching. Someone who worked in public relations and briefed reporters about the mayor's work definitely has communication skills to stand up in front of people and deliver information. This is a transferable skill. Insurance agents "teach" clients all the time. This is considered one-on-one teaching. List that experience.

Examples for a recent college graduate:

Work Experiences:

Lifeguard, Jacksonville Public Pool, summers, 2011, 2012

- Taught swim lessons to 8- to 14-year-olds

Aerobics instructor, Henley Dorm, Grant College, 2010–2012

• Led classes twice a week for groups of 24

Work Experiences:

Morgan Valley Bank, summers, 2010–2013

• Teller, 35 hours a week
• Led bank tours for preschool and elementary field trips

Window cashier, Raney College, four semesters, 12 hours a week

Examples for a career changer:

Work Experiences:

Public Relations Director, City of Carsonville, Idaho, 2005–2007
    Assistant Public Relations Director, 2003–2005

• Wrote press releases and edited speeches
• Organized and taught town meetings
• Served as liaison to county committees and county board

Editor, *Clark College Herald*, 2000–2001

• Supervised production and editing
• Directed a staff of seven students

Work Experiences:

Assistant Customer Service Director, Main Street Bank, Carroll, GA, 2006–2009

Cashier, Main Street Bank, 2004–2006

• Scheduled hours for seven cashiers
• Taught orientation sessions for new hires
• Provided one-on-one counseling for customers

What should I do about having 15 or 20 years of work experiences before I moved into teaching? Summarize this work experience succinctly. For example:

Work Experiences:

Fifteen years of experience in restaurant management, including

- Applebee's, Manager, 2011–2013, supervising 34 employees
- McDonald's, Assistant Manager, 2009–2011, supervising 22 employees
- Hardee's, Assistant Manager, 1998–2009, supervising 12 employees

Stop and write out your work experiences. Emphasize work that demonstrates skills related to teaching—organizing, leading, explaining, and writing.

Professional memberships, special skills, awards, service, and leadership

You will name this section based on what you list here. For recent graduates, an employer is looking to see if you excelled in any areas in college, as past behavior is the best predictor of future behavior. A college student who was named to two honor societies and who served as a club president demonstrates high achievement and leadership. Joining a professional association as a college student indicates professionalism.

Teachers with experience should list their professional memberships and leadership roles taken in previous jobs. These might include committee chairmanships, directing tutoring programs, or presentations at PTA/PTO meetings.

Teachers who have stopped out of their careers may include leadership roles in community organizations or their children's schools. Being a classroom volunteer, or organizing a library fundraiser, indicates ongoing work with schools while stopping out to raise one's own small children.

Examples for a recent graduate:

Professional Memberships, Awards, and Leadership

- Inducted into Kappa Delta Pi International Honor Society, spring 2011
- Kappa Delta Pi chapter vice-president, fall 2012
- Dean's list, seven semesters
- Future teacher scholarship recipient, junior and senior years

Examples for an experienced teacher:

Memberships, Service, Leadership

- Phi Delta Kappa, 2009–present

- International Reading Association, 2009–present
- Chair, countywide curriculum committee on 3rd grade literacy test, 2011
- Assistant director, after-school enrichment series, fall 2010
- Grant recipient, $200, "Build a class library"

Skills, Leadership, Memberships

- Fluent in Spanish; working knowledge of French
- Member of National Middle School Association
- Served on district task force for at-risk students
- Served on principal's committee for evaluation of 7th grade test scores
- Directed "What Is Your Child Studying?" program, attended by 300 parents

Write out your areas of service, leadership, memberships, and awards. Next, narrow that list to the most important four to five items. Add this list to your resume.

References or Credentials

At the end of the resume, you may list three to four references with contact information. These must be people who have given their permission to serve as references. You may also add a line that states that your letters of recommendation will be sent by your college's career center in a credentials file.

To prepare this section, decide on the people who will serve as your references. Ask them well in advance of when you will need letters. See if your college offers a credentials file, either online or on paper. If the college offers the service, take advantage of it.

How articulate should my chosen references be? Some classroom teachers excel at working with children but are not good communicators by telephone or email. If you are concerned about this, choose other references.

Should you include a well-known name in the community as a reference? Some people like to use their mayor, their state representative, or a well-known superintendent or school board president as a reference. This may work for you, provided that the person really does know your work as a teacher.

Recent graduates should always include the teacher with whom they worked in student teaching and a college supervisor. Teachers with experience should use former supervisors, including department chairs, grade-level lead teachers, and principals.

What do employers want to hear from references? They want to know that you have been successful in the classroom. The best references are people who have seen you teach and who have evaluated your work.

Take all of your samples from this chapter, and create a resume with this blank activity sheet.

ACTIVITY SHEET: YOUR TEACHING RESUME

<u>Complete contact information</u>

<u>Professional Profile or Objective or Summary of Qualifications</u> (one to two lines)

<u>Certification/Licensure</u> (if not clearly stated in above)

<u>Education</u>

<u>Teaching Experience</u>

<u>Other Work Experiences</u>

<u>Professional Memberships, Special Skills, and Awards OR Service and Leadership</u>

<u>References and/or Credentials Available</u>

SAMPLE RESUMES

The following resumes are all fictional. Candidate names, cities, and colleges have been invented. Any name or college that appears real is purely coincidental.

You will see that some resumes have a different format than others. Some have different uses of capital letters. This is because there is no one right way to write a resume. Often, capital letters are used just for emphasis, not because a noun is a proper noun. Of course, proper nouns must be capitalized.

As you create your resume, and show it to people for feedback and editing, you will get differing opinions. This, too, is normal. Listen to the feedback and then decide for yourself.

SAMPLE RESUME FOR A NEW ELEMENTARY TEACHER

Carol Anthony Walker

Contact Information:

111 Main Street, Cartersville, NC, 23456

Email: carolwal@sample.com Phone: (123) 456-7890

Professional Profile: Fully certified in elementary education, with a type 04 North Carolina certificate, I completed student teaching that included 16 weeks in an urban district. Recipient of the College of Education Founder's Award, I have completed eight additional hours in reading diagnosis and literacy.

Education: BA, Elementary Education, North Carolina State, 2013

- 3.4 GPA; one semester at North Carolina's exchange program in Vancouver, BC

Teaching Experience: Winston Elementary School, Winston, NC, spring 2013

- Student teaching, 3rd grade, 27 students, including seven special needs
- Taught full-time for three weeks; implemented "Caring Discipline"
- Designed and delivered units on high-impact reading and mathematics
- Supervised the North Carolina 3rd grade standards test

Columbia Elementary School, Columbia, NC, fall 2012

- 70-hour field experience with 1st and 2nd grade literacy classes
- Taught 6 reading lessons to classes with 25–31 students
- Graded pre-tests for the writing intensive project

Mountain Primary School, Columbia, NC, fall 2011–spring 2012

- 50-hour field experience with 4th grade
- Tutored reading and science lessons
- Taught three whole-group lessons in reading

Other Work Experiences: Assistant Librarian, Winslet Public Library, Winslet, NC

- Summers, 2010, 2011, 2012; led reading circles for 8- to 12-year-olds
- Assisted lead librarian with summer reading program and book sale

Library assistant, North Carolina State, fall 2010–fall 2012

- Worked up to 15 hours a week in research and at front desk

Professional Memberships, Awards, and Service

Member, Kappa Delta Pi International Honor Society, 2011–present

- Served as chapter treasurer and secretary
- Attended the 2011 Convocation, Indianapolis, as a poster presenter

Member, International Reading Association, 2011–present

- College of Education Founder's Award for overall achievement, 2013
- Dean's list, five semesters
- Volunteer, "North Carolina Feeds Its Neighbors" food drive, 2012, 2013

References

Dr. Candy Stegen, college supervisor, North Carolina State
      Email: cstegen@sample.edu Phone: (123) 456-7890

Mrs. Mandy North, cooperating teacher, Winston Elementary School
      Email: mnorth@sample.edu Phone: (123) 456-8901

Mrs. Mary Oates, cooperating teacher, Mountain Primary School
      Email: moates@sample.edu Phone: (123) 456-7892

Letters of recommendation will be sent via email to you from the Career Center, North Carolina State, www.careersamplenc.edu

SAMPLE RESUME FOR A NEW MIDDLE SCHOOL TEACHER

Sam Collins

Contact Information:

111 Randolph, Phoenix, AZ, 89123

Email: scoll@sample.net Phone: 345-678-9012

web site: www.samteaches@sample.net

Professional Profile: Having completed degrees in psychology and education, I am fully certified with a type 7 Arizona Middle Grades Certificate. My concentrations include science and language arts.

Education: BA, Middle Grades Education, Arizona College, Tempe, 2013

- BS, Psychology, Arizona State, Tempe, 2013
- 3.9 GPA; included a three-week May term in Costa Rica

Associate's Degree, Psychology, People's College, Tempe, AZ, 2010

- 3.2 GPA; included an internship in social services, spring 2010
- Six semesters of college Spanish completed

Teaching Experience: Lincoln Middle School, Phoenix, spring 2013

- Student teaching, 7th grade science, five classes daily, 115 students
- Designed and taught three units: biospheres, elements, and ecology
- Established a science web site for all 7th grade classes

Magellan Middle School, Phoenix, fall 2011–spring 2012

- Completed 80 practicum hours in language arts; 25 in science
- Taught two units—reading for you and reading test preparation
- Reviewed for and supervised the Arizona Language Arts 8th grade exam

Honors Middle School, Phoenix, spring 2010

- Observed and assisted 6th grade teacher with science classes (30 hours)
- Taught two lessons; completed developmental scans of five at-risk students

Work Experience: Psych Lab Student Director, Arizona College, 2010–2013

- Scheduled 18 student workers each semester
- Implemented an online recording system for work hours

Server and Weekend Manager, Sam's Barbeque, Tempe, AZ

- 2007–2010; worked 30 hours a week during school year; full-time summers
- Assisted in the creation of an online employee review program

Skills and Awards

- Completed six workshops on Mac and PC programs
- Working knowledge of Spanish
- Recipient, outstanding student worker award, Arizona College, 2012
- Recipient, Sam's Power Employee Award, 2009 ($2,000)

References

Mrs. Sarah High, 7th grade teacher, Lincoln Middle School
   Email: highs@sample.edu Phone: 345-678-9034

Dr. Mary Jones, college supervisor, Arizona College
   Email: jonesma@sample.edu Phone: 345-678-9056

Mr. Sam Henders, owner, Sam's Barbeque, Tempe
   Phone: 345-678-9078

SAMPLE RESUME FOR AN EXPERIENCED TEACHER

Ami Adams Richter

Contact Information:

76 Dunbar Avenue, Apt. 845, Miles City, Nevada, 87111

Email: aarichter@sample.com Phone: 678-901-2345

Professional Profile: With five years of experience teaching all levels of high school Spanish and a master's degree in education, I facilitate student learning and motivate students to graduate.

Certification: Type 07 Secondary Teaching Certificate, Spanish; Endorsements in ESL and French.

Education:

- MA, Curriculum and Instruction, Nevada State University, 2012; 3.8 GPA
- BA, Spanish, Trentor College, 2007, 3.4 GPA, included a semester at the University of Salamanca, Spain

Teaching Experience: Silver City High School, Nevada, 2007– present

- Teach four classes of Spanish daily; 9th–12th grades

Direct the ESL tutoring program

- Sponsored the Freshman Graduation Party, 2009, 2010, 2011 (a program to raise high school graduation rates)
- Featured speaker at parents' programs: "Your Child's College Education" and "How Does a Student Get Into the Right College?"

University High School, spring 2007

- Student teaching, 9th and 10th grades, 143 students daily

Taught two ESL classes for seven weeks

Additional Work Experience:

Student Travel Incorporated, summers 2009, 2010

- Leader of student trips in Ecuador, Peru, and Argentina

Rotary Youth Exchange, 2008–2010

- Taught weekend seminars for U.S. students chosen to study abroad
- Provided orientation for students arriving from Latin America

References:

Mrs. Tonya Bell, Principal, Silver City High School
    Email: principal@sample.edu Work phone: 543-210-9876

Mr. Silvio Herrera, Curriculum Director, Silver City District
 Email: silherr@sample.edu Phone: 543-210-9877

Mr. Paul Soares, Rotary President, Silver City
 Email: soares@sample.org Phone 543-678-9012

SAMPLE RESUME FOR A CAREER CHANGER

Sonia Menendez Arroyo

Contact Information:

11 Peyton Drive, Truesdale, GA 30123

Email: sonarroyo@gmail.com Phone: 765-432-1098

Professional Profile: With ten years of experience in retail sales, I bring real-world experience to the teaching of high school social studies.

Certification: GA 5 certificate for the teaching of social studies, grades 7–12. Endorsements in business education and technology.

Education: Teacher Certification Program, Mountain State University, Marietta, GA
 Spring, 2013, 4.3 GPA

- BA, Marketing, Mountain State University, spring 2000
- AA, Business, Evergreen Community College, spring 1998

Teaching Experience: Mountain City High School, Marietta, GA

- Student teaching, 10th and 11th grade American History, Civics, spring 2013
- Taught three units: World War II, Industrial Revolution, and Voting Rights
- Supervised high school graduation test
- Assisted with Junior Achievement business club

Fountain High School, fall 2012

- 65-hour field experience in high school civics class
- 25-hour field experience in 10th grade vocational technology class

- Taught ten lessons in civics; three in technology

Work Experience: Manager, Children's Department, Huering Family Store, Atlanta, GA, 2006–2011

- Supervised 18 employees

- Charged with purchasing all seasonal lines
- Represented the company on five buying trips to San Francisco; two to Hong Kong

Assistant Manager, Women's Wear, Macy's, Marietta, GA, 2000–2006

- Supervised 12 employees
- Managed annual budget of $850,000

Skills, Service, Memberships

- Fluent in Spanish
- Advanced skills in budget and finance
- Member, Phi Delta Kappa, 2012–present
- Employee of the year, Huring Family Store, 2009

References:

My credentials file, with four letters, will be sent by Mountain State University.

SAMPLE RESUME FOR A NEW SUBSTITUTE TEACHER

Patrice Hendalay

Contact Information:

111 Maple Road, Big Mountain, CO 99111

Email: hen1@sample.net Phone: 123-123-4567

Professional Profile: A former fast-food service manager, I bring organizational and motivational skills to substitute teaching.

Training: Colorado substitute teaching registration, 2013. Completed district-level training in Big Mountain District 13 and Pine Log District 7, 2013.

Education: AA in Business, Fountain College, Big Mountain, CO

* 2.89 GPA, spring 2010

Wendy's Management Trainee Program Diploma, December 2010

Work Experience:

Substitute teacher and volunteer: Bright Star Day Care, Monroe, CO, January 2013–present

* Completed 20 days of substitute teaching and volunteering, three- to five-year-olds
* Worked with after-school program for 6- to 12-year-olds

Wendy's, Big Mountain, CO, January 2011–November 2012

* Assistant manager, both night and day shifts
* Scheduled 16 employees
* Trained 22 employees

Internship, Burger Winner, Big Mountain, CO, fall semester, 2010

* Worked 20 hours per week
* Completed "Young Manager's Winner Circle"

Skills, Service, Memberships

Advanced skills in Windows spreadsheets and online data management
Earned the state "New Manager Award" for people skills, Wendy's, 2012

References:

Mr. Don Butler, Field Representative, Western Wendy's
Email: db@sample.net Phone: 123-456-7890

Ms. Clarissa Martin, General Manager, Wendy's, Big Mountain
Email: cmartin@sample.net Phone: 567-890-1234

Mrs. Betty Smith, Instructor, Fountain College
Email: smithb@sample.edu Phone: 456-789-0123

Chapter Four

The Cover Letter

With so much of the hiring process being online, is a cover letter obsolete? No, you may still need one, and if you do, the content and style are very important. What is the use of the cover letter? The cover letter is a short narrative that introduces you, and your resume, to the potential employer. A traditional cover letter accompanies every paper copy of your resume and is NEVER over one page long. A cover letter includes:

1. One paragraph that introduces you to the reader and states the position or position for which you are applying
2. A paragraph that highlights your qualifications, experience, and background
3. A paragraph that states that you have applied, have had your letters of recommendation sent, and are ready to interview
4. One of the above paragraphs should state what you know about this district and why you want to work there

Other key points to remember when writing a cover letter include:

1. Do not send a cover letter addressed to sir or madam. You should read the job ad and find a person to whom the letter should be addressed.
2. Do not use a small font or single-spacing to get more information in the letter. Use a 12-point font and 1½ or double-spacing. You must be succinct. Often a staff person is pre-sorting cover letters and resumes to ascertain your certification status and work experience, and they simply will not read a letter that is too long or in a small or unusual font. Neither will an administrator who is reading the letters and resumes.

3. Sign your name legibly. This is quite important, as your future employer needs to know that you can write legibly. An employer sees your signature and thinks, "Will a parent complain if a letter goes home and the teacher's signature is illegible?" Principals try to avoid parent complaints about everything.
4. The cover letter is only one page long. Do not include everything. Your cover letter and your resume combined should give a clear, succinct picture.

ACTIVITY SHEET FOR WRITING A COVER LETTER

Your complete mailing address, phone, email

Name of the individual to receive the letter, and title

Complete mailing address

Salutation, Mr./Ms. Last name

First paragraph:

- An opening line about your certification/qualifications
- The job for which you are applying and where you found the job ad

Second paragraph:

- Lead with your strengths/your best teaching experience
- Describe a career highlight
- Talk about your impact on raising student achievement/test scores

Third paragraph:

- What you know about the district
- Your interest in the district
- State that your application and all paperwork have been completed

Sign legibly with black ink.

SAMPLE COVER LETTER FOR A NEW GRADUATE

123 West Valley Rd.
Jamestown, VA 12345

Phone: 345-678-9012

Email: student@sample.com

Ms. Pam Ebhert, Personnel Director
Jamestown City Schools
211 West 2nd Street
Jamestown, VA 12345

Ms. Ebhert:

Having recently completed my BA in music with teacher certification at Highland College, I am delighted to learn of the opening for a vocal music teacher in your district. Your district made the news last year for its glee club, and I would love to be a part of its continued success.

My experience includes a semester of student teaching in nearby Glouster Consolidated High School, as well as 60 hours of field experience in Powder Canyon's music program. I know the excitement and sense of confidence that glee club brings to high school students, as I was lucky enough to sing with Hampton High's club the year that we placed second in the state. My professional goal is to bring the power of music to all of my future students.

I have completed your district's online application and have also sent the required paperwork to your office. The college career center will send my credentials packet with letters of recommendation within ten days. I may be reached with the contact information provided above, and I look forward to the opportunity to interview—and even sing—in your district.

Sincerely,

Your Name

SAMPLE LETTER FOR A TEACHER WITH EXPERIENCE

11 Lavendar Lane
Smithfield, GA 12345

Phone: 345-678-9012

Email: gteacher@sample.com

Mr. Peter Hampton, Assistant Superintendent
Grace Meadows School District
123 Main Street
Horton, GA 34567

Mr. Hampton:

Please accept this letter and the enclosed resume as part of my application for the position of elementary teacher in your district, as advertised on your web site. With seven years of experience teaching grades 3 and 4, I feel that I have developed a strong set of skills for raising student achievement.

My classroom has always been one that runs smoothly because of taught procedures and routines. My management plan is posted, sent home to parents, and taught to students during the first two weeks of school. With strong management skills in place, my classroom is both business-like and pleasant. We get things done, as evidenced by my students' scores on the GA CRCT test. My students have consistently scored above the state average for the last five years. My classroom web site, with homework hints, is available at www.mywebsite.edu.

My application packet, including online materials, is complete. Since your district is very similar to the one where I currently work, in size and student demographics, I look forward to the opportunity to share my experience with your students. Thank you in advance for your consideration.

Sincerely,

Your Name

SAMPLE LETTER FOR A CAREER CHANGER

11 Maple Street
Georgetown, VT 06544

Phone: 456-789-0987

email: grantw@sample.net

Ms. Susan Trentor, Supervisor of Hiring
Longbranch School District
27 Education Street
Hamilton, VT 06124

Ms. Trentor:

Having just finished an MAT program at Vermont State, with teacher certification in middle grades language arts, I am thrilled to apply for the position at Longbranch Middle, as advertised on teachVT.com. I bring twelve years of experience as a newspaper editor and journalist to the teaching profession and hope to instill a love of writing in all of my students.

As a professional writer, I can teach my students the skills needed in today's workplace. I will bring the real world into the classroom, sharing the work ethic needed to get, and keep, a job in today's tough economy. My student teaching experience taught me that it takes more than content skills to become a teacher. I learned management skills and the psychology behind a middle-schooler's mind by working with a wonderful mentor teacher for five months.

My application materials have all been forwarded to your office. I look forward to an opportunity to interview for this position and to meet other teachers in your award-winning district. Winning the 2011 Dewey prize is a great accomplishment, and I would love to be a part of your district's future.

Sincerely,

Your Name

SAMPLE COVER LETTER FOR AT-RISK STUDENT POPULATIONS

12 Logan Dr.
Alexandria, MI 44411

Phone: 123-456-7890

email: anystudent@sample.net

Mr. Paul Roberts, Assistant Director of Personnel
Goodard County Schools
123 Apple Rd
Brighton, WI 34111

Mr. Roberts:

Please accept this letter and my resume for the advertised positions in secondary English in your district. Fully certified in both English and social studies, my experience includes a semester of student teaching in the Smithfield District, at Mable Alternative School, and a year of substitute teaching in that school. The Mable School is an urban school for at-risk students, and the successes at that school are known throughout our state.

As a substitute teacher, I was a full-time employee, and my duties varied on a daily basis from teaching English in grades 9–12, to supervising a study hall for those students assigned to school instead of jail. This experience has prepared me for the student population of your school district, and I possess the management skills to reach out to the most needy of students. The students at Mable, just as your students in Goodard County, are capable of great success, but first we must win their trust and increase their basic academic skills.

I would appreciate the opportunity to interview in your district. My experiences over the last two years have prepared me to teach and have also deepened my commitment to reach out to all students, providing hope and skills for them to succeed in the world.

Thank you in advance for your consideration.

Sincerely,

Your Name

ONLINE LETTERS AND NETIQUETTE

If no paper copies accompany an application for a teaching job, are online communications, such as emails, important? Yes, all online communications are evaluated for their tone, grammar, and spelling. Every email that you send to a district administrator, or staff person, should be professional. Good etiquette for online writing is called "netiquette" (Clement, 2010) and includes the following:

1. Use titles when addressing anyone in an email. Do not start an email with "hey" or "hi." Address messages to Mr. Roberts, Director of Personnel, for example.
2. Make your email message look like a formal letter. Do not use abbreviations or make a message all one paragraph. Your written work in an email message is being judged, just as your paper cover letter would be. Professional teachers use professional language in all communications.
3. Have someone read your message, or your electronic cover letter, before you push send. Letters should be proofread, whether submitted on paper or electronically.
4. Spelling and grammar always matter. Always.

Chapter Five

The Interview Portfolio

All teachers know the value of visual aids. An interview portfolio is a visual aid. This portfolio is NOT a scrapbook, nor is it like the portfolios most student teachers are required to make to evidence program completion. The portfolios used to document standards in a teacher education program require cover sheets that explain the items (called artifacts). These portfolios are usually graded and are often huge in size, filling a three-inch binder or taking up a lot of space in electronic form. (See, for example, Campbell et al., 2011; Costantino, De Lorenzo, and Tirrell-Corbin, 2008.)

So, how is an interview portfolio different? First, it is small. It contains only a few items, and each item can be used to answer an interview question. An interview portfolio must include:

1. A classroom management plan
2. A parent letter
3. One or two sample lesson plans
4. One or two pages of a unit plan or curriculum map
5. A sample quiz or exam, created by the candidate
6. Evidence of student achievement
7. Student work samples
8. A few pictures of a well-organized classroom

The interview portfolio fits into a half-inch or one-inch binder. The portfolio has tabs so that the candidate can find each item quickly when referring to it. The portfolio is paper, not electronic, as it is used as a visual aid at job fair interviews and on-site interviews. I discuss electronic portfolios and online web sites that showcase work later on in the chapter.

Guidelines for the creation of an interview portfolio:

1. All pages must be typed and be extremely neat.
2. Sheet protectors should be used on each page, since the portfolio will be used many times.
3. Tabs should be large, typed, and easy to use.
4. There should be no student names or any identifying references.
5. There should be no pictures of students. You never know who will see the pictures, and in order to use student photos you need express written consent of the parents.
6. Photos can be of the classroom, without students, and should be ones that help you to explain classroom organization, routines, and procedures.

KEY: Interviewers rarely ask to see your portfolio. You will use the portfolio to explain your answers to questions about classroom management, communication with parents, lesson planning, long-range planning, and student achievement. The items in the portfolio should address these topics.

SAMPLE PORTFOLIO ITEMS

The best portfolio items are ones that you have used in your field experience, student teaching, or previous teaching position. When you have used an item, you can then explain what you did and what you learned by doing it.

A strong answer follows. "Here is a lesson plan that I taught to 8th grade students. It went well because I planned a focus about the upcoming elections. Then, I had a brainstorming activity. When I delivered the new material, they were prepared to ask questions, and they were also prepared to answer questions. A short reading reinforced what I had already presented, and then they wrote two paragraphs about running for office." Since the candidate has the lesson in the portfolio, and is showing it, it is much easier to answer the question. Again, the portfolio is a visual aid.

The following are samples of pages that you can create, if you do not already have examples from your student teaching or past classroom teaching experience. Following the samples are ideas for other portfolio pages.

SAMPLE CLASSROOM MANAGEMENT PLAN, 5TH GRADE

Rules

1. Keep hands, feet, and objects to yourself.
2. Use only appropriate language.

3. Follow all directions.
4. No interrupting or loud discussions.
5. Be in your seat or in the appropriate area for an activity.

Consequences/Corrective Actions

1. Verbal reminder
2. Two minutes away from class at side of room
3. Completion of self-management sheet
4. 20-minute detention
5. Parent phone call and/or office referral

Positive Supports

1. Verbal support
2. Time earned for reading or computer
3. Positive postcard (to take home)
4. Participation in Principal's Reward Program

The teacher may skip early steps for a major infraction that could harm any other student in the room.

SAMPLE PARENT LETTER
(FOR THE BEGINNING OF A SCHOOL YEAR)

Dear Families and Guardians,

Welcome to ninth grade language arts! High school is different than middle school, as we begin the process of preparing students for college, meaningful work, and their lives after graduation. Yes, even in ninth grade we talk a lot about high school graduation and the skills that all students need for the future.

Our curriculum focuses on the following big topics, which are based on the national Common Core Standards and our state's performance standards:
(list big topics here)

Many parents ask how they can help their children learn in high school. I suggest that they talk with their children regularly about the readings from class. Read your children's papers and assignments. Ask about test grades. I will post assignments at www.anytownhila.edu, and you can check this site weekly for updates. I will also send out a curriculum guide or syllabus every nine weeks.

My next letter will be about classroom management and parent conferences, which will be held October 8–9.

I appreciate opportunities to talk with my students' parents. I can be reached by email at mserin@sample.com, or by phone at 567-098-0022 between 3:15 and 4:00. Messages may be left by voicemail.

I look forward to a great year with your child.

LESSON PLAN

2nd grade language arts

Wed., April 2

Standards: LA12A and B; using nonfiction for reading and factual knowledge

Goals: The teacher will (TTW) introduce the production and use of potatoes.
TTW read the book *Paulie's Potato Farm* with students.

Objectives: The students will (TSW) be able to list three steps in growing potatoes.
TSW be able to tell the difference between fiction and nonfiction in the book read.

Focus: Name the ways that you have eaten potatoes (French fries, baked potato, tater tots, etc.). TTW list all the answers on Smartboard.

Introduction: Using a chart to write out what students know about potatoes, TTW list what they know (K), then what they want to know (W), and leave a column for what they learned (L).

Body of lesson:

1. TTW read *Paulie's Potato Farm*, with students reading and repeating key phrases.
2. New words will be listed on chart paper.
3. After reading the book, the teacher asks students what they learned, and the W and L columns of the chart are completed.
4. Students complete independent work about growing potatoes.

Assessment: TTW grade reading review sheet for completion and inclusion of six vocabulary words.

Conclusion: What's for lunch today? Let's read the menu (tater tots). How did those tater tots get to our school cafeteria?

Reflection: TTW write out how the lesson went, with changes for next time. How do we know that the students' met the standards? What will the summative assessment be later in the week?

SAMPLE UNIT OR CURRICULUM MAP

These will vary widely. Some unit plans look like lesson plans, with objectives, material to be covered, student learning experiences, and assessments summarized. The key is that the unit plan should be no more than two pages and should cover about two weeks of material.

Curriculum maps vary in their content and organization, as well. Some maps cover an entire semester in two pages, with the listing of big topics and the number of weeks per topic. Other maps include standards, objectives, student learning experiences, and a variety of assessments.

Again, a map should have only one or two pages. It is a sample of how you organize large amounts of information to be taught to students. It indicates your ability to do long-range planning and to meet the mandated curriculum in your state/district.

SAMPLE QUIZ, EXAM, OR RUBRIC

It is critical that a teacher know how to assess student learning. Including one original quiz, exam, or rubric gives you a visual aid when asked about assessing student work. Additionally, you may want to add a page about how students' work is graded.

Ninth Grade English Grading System

In this class, every assignment, quiz, test, or project is given a numeric score. Each time you get a grade, you can record it and have a summary of exactly what your grade is at any time during the nine weeks.

How points are earned:

Homework is spot-checked or graded for 5 to 20 points.
Projects and major papers are worth 20 to 40 points.
Quizzes are worth 10 to 30 points.
Tests range from 60 to 100 points.

When your grades are totaled, your earned points are divided by the number of points possible. For example:

5/5, 12/15, 19/20, 22/25, 32/40, 10/10, 20/25, 55/60, 72/85

Your total = 247 points earned

Possible points = 285

247/285 = 86%

    90–100% = A
    80–89% = B
    70–79% = C
    60–69% = D
    0–59% = F

EVIDENCE OF STUDENT ACHIEVEMENT

Employers want to know that you have impacted student achievement in a positive way. How can you evidence your impact on student achievement? Many student teachers are required to do some pre-testing of students, followed by teaching a lesson and then post-testing. They summarize the results in a table that keeps student identities anonymous. For example:

$n = 22$
Pre-test scores for verb unit: mean score, 45%
Post-test scores for verb unit: mean score, 88%
Sample test included

Teachers with experience may include samples of standardized test scores for past classes, with short explanations. Again, all student and school identifiers should be removed.

    Your sample of impacting student achievement can be a powerful piece of evidence in the interview portfolio. Be prepared to share how you have helped raise student achievement when asked.

STUDENT WORK SAMPLES AND PICTURES

If you have worked with students on a particularly unique project or assignment, you may add a sample of student work from the project, with the name removed. Do not put a large sample in the portfolio, but one that is one to two pages. Never put a sample in one sheet protector if the reader would have to pull the sample out to read the material. There should be a sheet protector for every page, and the reader just turns the pages.

Pictures of your classroom should be limited to ones that evidence your experience in organizing classroom space. Pictures help you to answer questions about classroom organization, routines, and procedures. Remember that an interview portfolio is not a scrapbook, and that the purpose of each sample in the portfolio is to support your verbal answers to interview questions.

FAQs About Portfolios

1. If my portfolio is only five or six items, should I make enough copies to leave with interviewers? No, this is not necessary. Your portfolio is your visual aid and you use it while answering questions.
2. If an interviewer does not ask to see my portfolio, should I be concerned? Interviewers generally do not ask to see the portfolio. You share it when appropriate. You do not say, "Here is my portfolio," or "Can I show you my portfolio now?"
3. In interviews that I have been on in the past, I have been seated across from the employer. How do I turn the portfolio for them to see? Show the portfolio so that they are able to read it; you can read upside down because you are so familiar with the content.
4. My college supervisor said that as a new teacher, just finishing student teaching, that my three-inch binder with all of the work from my senior year would really impress an employer. Is she right? As with all aspects of the job search, you will hear differing opinions from those who advise you. Generally, large binders that evidence your mastery of teacher education standards are too cumbersome to be used in job interviews.
5. Should I put a copy of my resume in my portfolio? You may, but you don't really need to, because you will carry extra copies of your resume with you to job fairs and interviews.

Online and Electronic Portfolios

In many teacher education programs, candidates complete electronic portfolios as they progress through their programs. A final electronic portfolio includes lessons taught, evaluations by teachers in field experiences, student work samples, a philosophy of education statement, evidence of experience with diverse student populations, and all required paperwork for teacher certification. This type of portfolio is posted on a protected web site, accessible by the professors who will grade the portfolio.

If you choose to take your education program electronic portfolio and put it on a flash drive or disc, you may do so. However, in an interview situation, employers will not have time to read these materials, and employers will not need to see all of the materials you created over several years in your program.

Both new and practicing teachers can create a web site with sample lesson plans, teacher-created materials, a management plan, and pictures of an organized classroom. There might be PowerPoint presentations or a video clip of the teacher presenting new material. Practicing teachers can direct employers to their current classroom web site or blog. Candidates who share this type of online information post their web site address on their resume, near the top, after the professional profile. The line reads: Lesson plans and teaching materials available for view at (list site). KEY points for online posts include:

1. You may not use student photos without the express written consent of parents. It is better to NOT include any photos with students at all.
2. You may only post original materials. It has to be your PowerPoint, and any music or photos in the presentation must be used only with the correct permissions.
3. Your web site or blog must be a good one, with positive samples. If used, it should be a showcase of your teaching. It must be professional.
4. Do not reveal too much personal information on your site. Never be negative in a blog or refer to specific students, former students, or other teachers or administrators.

For more information, go to www.teachnet.com/how-to/employment/portfolios/index.html and www.best-job-interview.com/teacher-portfolio.html.

Your Total Online Presence

It is easy for administrators to do an online search for you. They may check Facebook or any other social media site. What do these sites say about you? How much of your social presence is available for anyone to see? Take the time to do a search of yourself. Check your sites and "clean" them up as needed. The same is true for your voicemail message. If you are a professional, your voicemail message should reflect that.

Chapter Six

Applying for Jobs

HOW JOBS GET ADVERTISED

Teaching positions are advertised in multiple ways. In some cases, the school district's teachers' union/association may have a contract stating how openings are first posted internally for a certain amount of time, before a public announcement is made. If a district has experienced a reduction in its teaching force, contracts may state that no job will be advertised as open until all recently released teachers have had the opportunity to apply.

These stipulations aside, there are national, commercial sites that post job openings. These sites earn money by charging the employer for the advertisement and other services, and do not charge the job candidates. Do a web search for teaching jobs, and multiple sites will appear, or start with one of the following:

www.teachers-teachers.com
www.schoolspring.com
www.k12jobs.com
www.educationamerica.net
www.wanttoteach.com

In addition to commercial sites, many professional associations provide an online career center. These sites may list job openings and/or tips for job searching. A sample includes:

www.theteachersguide.com/Educationassociations.html
www.kdp.org/teachingresources/careercenter.php

Examples in specific fields include:

> www.ncte.org/career (English)
> www.nctm.org (math)
> www.actfl.org (foreign languages)
> www.reading.org (reading)

NATIONAL, STATE, AND DISTRICT JOB SITES

State-by-State Listings

Each state has its own web site for advertising jobs within that state. Do a search for your state and teaching jobs, to find the applicable site. Or, go to one of the following for that information:

> www.education.uky.edu/AcadServ/content/employment
> www.allteachingjobs.com
> www.kdp.org/teachingresources/tr/certification.php

District Web Sites/Local Postings

District web sites contain more complete job directions. Do a web search for the name of the district and then go to the "career opportunities" section. Of course, each district web site may have a different name for its section on job openings.

Do districts ever advertise their openings in newspapers anymore? The answer to this question is "rarely." Because most districts require an online application, little is done to advertise in local newspapers. However, there are always exceptions, so you can check the want ads for education positions. A district is more apt to advertise for staff positions in a local newspaper, or to advertise for paraprofessionals and substitute teachers in that venue.

HOW TO APPLY

The best advice about applying for a job is to apply exactly as the job advertisement states. Read all instructions before completing an application, and follow them.

How do you get a job application for a position? Go to the district's web site. The web site will provide an online application, or will provide instructions for the completion of a paper application. Some applications cannot be viewed until the candidate establishes an account with a login and password. Keep track of your logins and passwords so that you may go back to the site and check on your application status. Do not expect a district to answer your questions by phone or email if the information is provided online. Calling or emailing a district or building administrator or staff person with an application question only shows that you do not know how to follow instructions, or that you are very insecure. Either way, administrators will not want to hire you.

INFORMATION NEEDED ON AN APPLICATION

While every application varies, there are common items on most applications. Gather this information in a folder (online and on paper) so that you are ready to complete any district's application. On average, a district application is six to ten pages in length and must be word-processed.

Many applications require a handwritten answer to a question or require a handwritten autobiography. Why? The first reason is that administrators want to hire teachers with legible handwriting. The second reason is that they want to know the answer to the question asked. Do not type a response if requested to complete a handwritten response. Of course, you will have to then scan the written section into your online application. Just as with cover letters, when you sign an application, your signature must be legible. Your signature is judged by administrators, and a flamboyant chicken scratch is not received well by many future employers.

Key Hint: Do not leave required fields blank, as this is considered an incomplete application and will be placed in the "no consideration" pile (or the wastebasket). Blanks on an application are red flags that something is not right in your preparation or past experience.

Information Needed to Complete a Job Application

1. Complete contact information may include secondary contact information for new graduates who anticipate leaving campus soon
2. Social security number
3. Proof of eligibility to work in the United States born in the United States/U.S. passport number/green card
4. Position desired
5. Education background often includes ALL colleges and universities attended
6. High school information/date of graduation and location of high school
7. Professional certifications earned, dates and specific certificate title
8. Endorsements earned, including those for coaching
9. Date and location of student teaching

Questions About Certification and Past Employment

1. Have you ever lost a professional teacher certification?
2. Have you ever been terminated by a school district or put on suspension?
3. Have you received a dishonorable discharge from the military?

Ethics Questions

1. Have you been convicted of an offense relating to drugs or alcohol?
2. Have you been convicted of any other criminal offense? Explain.

Work Experiences—In Education and in Other Fields

1. List dates, exact names of employers, cities, states
2. Honors, awards, distinctions earned
3. Special interests or hobbies
4. Areas that you would like to coach or direct
5. List your references and their complete contact information
6. Proof of criminal background check
7. Handwritten answer to a question or a handwritten autobiography
8. Your legible signature
9. A copy of your resume
10. A cover letter

LETTERS OF REFERENCE

It takes professors and supervisors time to write your letters of recommendation, so start asking for these letters months before you need them. Check with your college or university to see if a credentials file is offered to you through the college career center. If it is, use it. When you use a credentials file, each letter writer completes one letter on your behalf and sends it to the career center. Each time that you apply for a job, you contact the center (usually online) to have all of your letters sent to a potential employer. This way, if you apply for dozens of jobs, your writers only write one letter.

To help your writers, consider the following:

1. Provide an addressed and stamped envelope so that the writer does not have to provide this.
2. Give the writer the most recent copy of your resume, so that he/she does not write incorrect information about you.
3. Allow the writer at least two weeks to complete the letter.

4. Thank the writer!
5. Always ask the person for the contact information that they want you to provide the employer. Employers do contact references, and the correct contact information is essential.

Some college career centers allow candidates to review their letters of recommendation. Before establishing a credentials file, find out if this is possible. If your college does not offer the credentials file service, then ask people to serve as your references on job applications, and do not ask them to write an individual letter unless one is needed by the district. It is not helpful for you to include several letters of reference with a job application if they are not requested. Also, many employers will not accept letters of reference sent by the candidate, as they need the letter sent directly by the writer or the college career center.

FAQS ABOUT DELIVERING A JOB APPLICATION PACKET

1. Some people say that the best way to get noticed is to deliver the application and all supporting materials in person to a school district. Is this best?

   This is rarely helpful. In large districts, a front office staff person will simply take the envelope and put it in a box with all of the letters received via regular mail. In many cases, an office staff person will instruct you not to give them the paperwork, as only applications sent online are accepted. If this is the case, you may have actually hurt your chances by being a pest and not following directions.
2. I will apply to a district as their directions state, but then I want to hand deliver my cover letter and resume to an individual building principal. Will that help me to get noticed?

   While there are many opinions on this, the answer is often no. Some applications state that "Applicants are requested to refrain from contacting principals and requesting an appointment or interview." Besides, you work for a district, not an individual school, and delivering a resume to one elementary school does not mean that the school would be the one where you would work, if hired. Principals do not like overly assertive candidates.

In some small districts, or in some private schools, principals are willing to accept walk-in candidates and will read their paperwork. Do not overstay your welcome if you do deliver paperwork in person. Be professionally dressed and keep your visit very short. Remember that if this principal goes around the central administration's guidelines on hiring, what else might he/she be doing "around" the guidelines?

Chapter Seven

Behavior-Based Interviewing, Illegal, and Crazy Questions

WHAT EMPLOYERS WANT

As concerned as job seekers are about getting jobs, school administrators are equally concerned about hiring high-quality new teachers who can do their jobs well. What do employers really want when they make a new hire?

1. A fully certified teacher who does not need remediation or special assistance to achieve success in the classroom.
2. A teacher who gets students to work quickly in each class, who keeps students engaged in appropriate work, and who can manage the classroom.
3. A teacher who is organized, and who plans thorough lessons and units for the students.
4. A teacher who can effectively assess and grade student work.
5. A teacher who can raise test scores and/or raise student achievement.
6. A teacher who is respected by other faculty members, and who "fits in." This is also called being a "team player."
7. A dependable employee who will be at school with minimum days out of the classroom.
8. A teacher who does not have student or parent complaints about his/her grading, homework, lectures, attire, or demeanor.
9. A teacher who is professional in dress, speech, and behavior.
10. A teacher who is willing to accept new duties and to grow professionally.

11. A teacher who is positive, who doesn't complain, and who will work toward improvement if there is a problem.
12. A teacher who will represent the school well in the community.

Now, how do you prove that you are this person? The answer is by explaining your past experience, skills, and expertise in every interview.

In *Preparing for the Behavior-Based Interview*, Fitzwater (2001) wrote:

> Most employers today ask only job-related questions. The reason is twofold:
>
> 1. They need to determine if you fill the essential qualifications of the position.
> 2. The only questions allowed under today's strict employment laws are those related directly to the position. (p. 7)

Janz, Hellervik, and Gilmore (1986) discuss behavior description interviewing as a precursor to behavior-based interviewing. They stated that "the behavior description interview proceeds from a structured pattern of questions designed to probe the applicant's past behavior in specific situations, selected for their relevance to critical job events" (p. 3). In other words, when interviewing for a teaching job, you will be asked a structured set of questions to find out if you have the skills to teach.

Anthony and Coghill-Behrends (2010) wrote, "Employers are basically trying to find out one thing in the interview: are you the best person to help their students succeed?" (p. 123). How do employers find out if you are the best person? They ask behavior-based questions.

"A behavior-based question is one designed to probe your past behavior in similar situations. . . . By asking you these questions they are fairly certain that they will hear responses that can clue them in to behaviors you are likely to repeat" (Anthony and Coghill-Behrends, 2010, p. 124).

Behavior-based interviewing (BBI) is all about past experience. Built on the premise that past behavior is the best predictor of future performance, BBI-style questions are formed with phrases like, "tell me about a time when . . . ," "how have you . . . ," "what has been your approach to . . . ," and "describe how you have . . . " Knowledgeable interviewers create their questions by adding the topics of teaching to the phrase stems.

The topics that you should be ready to discuss in an interview are the skills needed to teach. These include:

1. Curriculum—standards, state and district guidelines
2. Planning—both lesson planning and long-term planning
3. Methods of teaching
4. Classroom management, organization, student behavior, and discipline

5. Differentiation of instruction/reaching all students
6. Teaching gifted, special needs, and at-risk students
7. Assessment and grading of students
8. Communication with parents, administrators, and community
9. Involvement in professional work, committees, and organizations
10. Professionalism and staying current in your discipline

WHAT BBI-STYLE QUESTIONS LOOK LIKE

A sample question for each of the topics listed above follows.

1. How have the Common Core Standards, and your state standards, guided your planning?
2. Describe your long-term planning for a nine-week period.
3. What are some methods that you have used for teaching _____?
4. Describe a classroom management plan that you have used and why it worked well.
5. How have you differentiated instruction to meet the needs of an individual student?
6. Tell about your experiences teaching at-risk students.
7. Describe a grading scale that you have used for _____?
8. How have you successfully communicated with parents?
9. Describe your involvement with school committees or professional organizations.
10. How have you kept up with trends in your discipline and teaching in general?

How to Answer Behavior-Based Interview Questions

Just knowing the questions that may be asked of you is not enough to prepare for an interview. You need to practice answers to possible questions. First, you need to write out some key phrases that you want to include in each answer. Think about some specific examples of your experience with the topic of the question. Then, prepare a short vignette of that experience.

A vignette is a very short story that highlights your work with the topic. You will need to stand in front of a mirror and practice answers. After practicing with a mirror, practice with friends and other teachers serving as interviewers. If you know an administrator, ask him/her to give you a mock interview. Perhaps your college career center can provide a mock interview. Yes, this practice is important. You do not want to lose a job because you were simply too nervous in an interview. Practicing takes away the nervousness.

To guide your answers, consider PAR. PAR stands for Problem, Action, and Result. If asked a question about a problem, or any challenging topic, you can phrase your answer around your experience with this problem, and talk about the action you took and the result of the action. In other words, have you experienced the problem, do you know what to do, and how did you reflect on the issue as a learning experience?

Example question: Describe your long-term planning for a semester.

PAR answer: During my first semester as a teacher, I knew that I had to cover a huge amount of content in my freshman classes (problem). I was given the state standards, but without guidelines on timing, learning experiences, or assessments, other than the end-of-course test in March. So, I developed a curriculum map, where each week was outlined on just one page (action). We made hypothetical maps in my curriculum class as a senior, so I used that model. I kept my one-page map out on my desk as I wrote daily plans, and it helped tremendously (result). Here is a sample page from my map (opening portfolio). The only thing I would change for next time would be to make a map with all of the teachers who teach the class. Group brainstorming could really help anyone new to a school.

Example question: How have you differentiated instruction to meet the needs of an individual student?

PAR answer: During student teaching, I taught a three-day unit on letter writing to my fourth graders. Because their writing and vocabulary levels varied widely (problem), I had to find a way to assist students in completing a whole letter. My teacher recommended tents. A tent is simply a piece of paper with written directions that sits on the student's desk while he/she is working on the assignment (action).

Some of the tents had basic reminders for the letter. Other tents had the reminder and more key words given to the student. The tent also helps to focus the student's attention. The final letters were much better written because of the prompts on the tents, and I decided which students needed which prompts (result). Yes, this takes a little more prep time, but it saves time in class.

The other mnemonic device that can guide your answers is STAR. STAR is very similar to PAR, with the letters representing Situation, Task, Action, and Result. STAR differs a little from PAR because it guides the candidate to answer any question, not just ones about problems.

Example question: How have you successfully communicated with parents?

STAR answer: When I began my student teaching experience, my cooperating teacher required me to write a letter to parents about who I was and what I would be teaching. I was the first student teacher that she had ever worked with, and it was a big class of students—24 sixth graders (situation). She told me how important it was to share curriculum and study skills with the parents in a newsletter that went out every three weeks (task). I sent the first one and was pleased to get eight responses. I sent the next letter via email as well as paper and got ten responses from parents (action).

Here is a copy of the second newsletter that explains when the standardized tests would happen and how parents could help students get psyched up but not stressed out. I have learned that even if only a few parents respond, I need to keep doing this, as it really makes a difference to have positive PR with parents (result).

Example question: How have you kept up with trends in your discipline and with teaching in general?

STAR answer: When I was a senior in college, I was invited to join a teachers' honor society, Kappa Delta Pi (situation). I joined and I have kept my membership so that I receive their publications and so that I have full access to their web site (task). I turn to the web site for teaching ideas and to find articles—it's an easy way to do research. I also maintain my membership in the NSTA, the National Science Teachers Association, as I get great ideas from their publications, too (action). As one of my college professors said, "Do you want to go to a doctor who graduated and never read any journals about advancements in medicine?" I want, and need, to know what's new so that I can help my students (result).

OLD-FASHIONED, NON–BBI-STYLE QUESTIONS

Of course, not all administrators have had training in how to ask BBI-style questions and may ask other, more random questions. Some administrators ask questions that they were asked back when they were interviewed to be a teacher. Here are some old questions that just keep appearing in some teacher job interviews. The key to answering these questions is to phrase your response with a BBI-style prompt of PAR or STAR. You will want to answer the question by explaining your past skills, training, and experience. Remember that no matter the question, the employer wants to know if you can successfully do the job of teaching. You need to explain your past experience as a predictor of your future performance. (See the following questions with suggested answers.)

1. Q: Tell me about yourself.

   A: Often used as an icebreaker, the employer does not want to know your life history. Answer with a positive teaching experience that sets you apart from other candidates, such as a year-long student teaching experience or a 15-week student teaching experience with at-risk students.

2. Q: Why do you want to be a teacher?

   A: Elementary education majors tend to answer this question by saying that they love children and high school teachers say that they love their subject matter. Every employer has already heard these answers, so try another one. Talk about how you have helped students improve their academic achievement, or discuss how you have helped students meet their goals.

3. Q: Where do you see yourself in five to ten years? Or, what are your long-term goals?

   A: While no one has a crystal ball to see into the future, it is good to talk about teaching as a career, not just a job. Don't overuse phrases such as "life-long learner," but do talk about your serious goals. A safe answer involves your plans to continue to improve your teaching skills and to help students.

4. Q: What events brought you to this interview?

   A: This question is really asking how you chose to become a teacher and how you earned teacher preparation. Talk about your preparation to teach.

5. Q: What do you bring to the table (to this job)?

   A: The interviewer wants to know what is unique or special about your abilities or teacher training. Describe a specific part of your preparation (ESOL, extra courses in math, reading, etc.). Don't hesitate to describe your successes with students. An interview is not the time to be shy or overly humble.

6. Q: What did you learn by reading our web site?

   A: Describe their school and district. All employers expect you to do your homework before an interview.

7. Q: Who was your best teacher and why?

   A: Describe a teacher who helped you succeed.

8. Q: Who has been the most influential person in your life?

   A: Again, answer with a positive, one-minute answer.

9. Describe your personality.

   Employers probably want to hear that you are persistent, hard-working, and committed to whatever you start. Think of an example from college or a previous job that would substantiate these qualities.

10. Q: What do you expect from your administrator?

A: It's always safe to talk about having open communication between teacher and administrator.

ANSWERING CRAZY INTERVIEW QUESTIONS

In 2011, on the teachers-teachers.com Facebook site, job seekers reported some of the unique questions that they were asked in interviews. Those posts inspired the following section. The key to answering crazy questions is to answer the question by talking about your teaching experience and skills.

1. Q: The "if you were a . . ." question. This type of question includes "if you were a cartoon character, who would you be and why?" It might be "if you were an animal," or "if you were an ice cream flavor." How do you answer?

   A: There is no one right answer, but this type of question is generally asked to see how you handle surprises. Think on your feet. "I would be Hobbes from Calvin and Hobbes, because his character was the voice of reason for Calvin, and teachers should be reasonable." "I would be chocolate ice cream, simply because it's my favorite. I would use this question on the interest inventory I would give seventh graders on the first day of school, because I know how important it is to get to know students—even their favorite ice cream flavors."

2. Q: What song best describes your life?

   A: To answer, talk about a song you like that has meaning. For example, "My favorite song is 'Climb Every Mountain' from *The Sound of Music.* Climbing every mountain is a figurative way of describing how I might teach—always searching out new strategies for teaching my students."

3. Some questions may seem crazy to you, but the interviewer has a reason for asking them. If you are asked to write a paragraph or short essay about any topic, like your philosophy of education, or an introduction to a letter home to parents, the interviewer is looking to evaluate your writing skills. This type of request is a way to see if your handwriting/printing is legible, and if you can spell and write coherent sentences without a laptop. So, write your essay and pay attention to your handwriting!

4. "If I were a fly on the wall of your past classroom, what would I have seen?" This question is really asking you to describe a classroom where you have worked. Your answer should stress the organization of the room and how you implemented routines and procedures. You might get extra credit on your answer if you can open your portfolio to

a picture of a room that you organized, and then explain why room arrangement is so important to good classroom management.

5. Q: What about questions that are totally "out there"?

    A: If asked if you can prepare meatballs, how would you answer? An answer might be, "Yes, of course, but I would make them out of vegetarian crumbles, because I know how important healthy eating is. I would also incorporate healthy eating ideas into appropriate lessons for my fourth graders." The idea is not to get flustered, but to turn the question around and give an answer that highlights something you know about teaching. A weak answer might be, "Why are you asking that? I won't be making meatballs in my high school literature classes." Confrontation is not necessarily a good thing in an interview!

6. Q: Why should I hire you instead of the 200 other applicants for this job?

    A: This question is asked quite frequently, and sometimes it is just, "Why should I hire you?" You should have an answer to this question, as it is not a crazy one. Consider what you bring to the job and your special background in the subject matter, student teaching, or other volunteer or service work.

ANSWERING CRAZY QUESTIONS ACTIVITY

Write out a creative answer that highlights something you know about teaching.

1. If you were a flower, which flower would you be, and why?
2. Write a six-line poem about yourself. (Remember, this is a test of handwriting and spelling.)
3. What movie is one of your favorites and why so?
4. Do you believe that there is life on Mars?
5. What else are you ready to tell me that I haven't asked about?

Hypothetical Questions

1. Q: If we gave you an unlimited budget, what would you buy and why?
    A: Describe books and resources you have used successfully in previous teaching.
2. Q: If a parent stops you in the mall to ask about his/her child's progress, what would you say?
    A: Be positive, but professional. Recommend a parent conference to discuss achievement in depth.
3. Q: If a child falls asleep in your class, what would you do?

A: The answer depends on the situation. Know each student and his/her needs.

4. Q: If a child were to call you a foul name, how would you respond?

   A: Talk about how this would be addressed in your management plan and by a schoolwide plan.

5. Q: If we were to change your teaching assignment the second week of school, how would you react?

   A: Professionally. Talk about being a team player.

Negative Questions

The key to answering negative questions is to describe the situation, emphasize the task or action taken, and then give a result or reflection. Your answer should stress what you learned and how you won't make the mistake again. Also, don't make yourself look too bad. Employers who ask these types of questions may not have had much training in how to ask a good, BBI-style question. However, as a candidate, you should phrase your answer with something positive from your past experience.

1. Q: What is your biggest weakness as a teacher?

   A: Sample: I don't know if it's truly a weakness or not, but I am very positive about every child. In student teaching, and in my long-term substitute position, I was teased by other teachers about my optimism. If optimism is a weakness, I will take the criticism and stay optimistic.

2. Q: What kinds of mistakes do you think you will make?

   A: Sample: With any new position, a teacher is probably going to make mistakes with the amount of time it takes students to learn something, whether it's how long one lesson will last or how long it will take for students to fully understand a topic. To compensate for this, I will always do formative assessments as I teach and allow time for both reviews and enrichment activities.

3. Describe a mistake you made in student teaching or your previous job and what you learned from it.

   Advice: Don't be too hard on yourself here. Also, share something that you learned that indicates your strengths.

   Sample: In student teaching I taught a unit on letter writing to third graders. I completely underestimated the time it would take them to write original letters. I learned that I should model more, use more visuals, and divide the task into more than one lesson. Learning something well, with depth, is much more important than just covering a topic.

ILLEGAL QUESTIONS

Everything in this chapter has directed candidates to answer questions about their preparation to teach, their classroom skills, and their experience. This section discusses illegal questions and what to do if you are asked an illegal question in an interview. Directing advice to employers about illegal, discriminatory questions, Deems (1994) wrote:

> Federal legislation states that you cannot base a hiring decision on anything other than bona fide occupational qualifications. This means that you cannot discriminate against an applicant because of age, sex, marital status, ethnic origin, religious preference, sexual preference, or disabilities. (p. 39)

As a job candidate, you cannot be asked a question about any of the topics listed above. Most employers know this. However, some employers persist in asking illegal questions. They may ask an illegal question as a follow-up to something you have said. For example, if you state that you seek a job in the district because your spouse has recently moved to the area for his/her job, the employer sometimes says, "and what does your spouse do?" This is completely illegal. While you may volunteer information about your spouse, children, or origin because you feel it helps your case for getting a job, an interviewer may NOT ask any type of follow-up question about the information you shared.

HINT: Be very careful about what you do share about your personal life. Some employers do not like to hire newlyweds, or those who live with their significant other, and the like. Talk about your professional skills, training, and experience.

Small talk is not just small talk. Sometimes a school secretary or support staff person will be in the room where you are waiting for an interview. They may think that they recognize you and ask something like, "Haven't I seen you at my church?" This is a completely illegal question. Everyone at a school is involved in hiring, and illegal questions may not be asked by the interviewer, the secretaries, the support staff, or even a student who walks you down a hall to an office. Other illegal "small talk" questions include:

Haven't I seen you at my son's day care?
What a pretty ring. Tell me about it.
I love the pattern and colors in your scarf. Do they mean something?
Do you live far from our building? Was your drive far?

What to Do When Asked an Illegal Question

When asked an illegal question, you have several options. You can, of course, answer the question. You can try to avoid it, or you can confront the employer about the question. Let's look at each option.

Some candidates choose to answer the question, in order to avoid confrontation during an interview. If asked about a spouse or children, you can choose to answer the question to your benefit. For example, "Yes, I am happily married. My spouse and I plan to make this community our permanent home, and that's another reason that I want to work in this district, helping to shape the education of all students in the community."

If asked about children, frame your response about how your own children have made you a better teacher. "Yes, I have two children, and since both are now in school, I see the parents' perspective on education. I know that I want to communicate with parents the way that I appreciate hearing from my children's teachers. Let me show you a sample newsletter that I sent out in my last job, and that is an example of how I will communicate with parents."

Some administrators try to ask the illegal questions in subliminal ways. An employer might say, "We want our teachers to be part of our school family. We have a back-to-school picnic and invite the employee and the families. Would your family enjoy this?" This is still illegal.

Is there a diplomatic way to say that you won't answer the question? Some candidates feel that they really shouldn't answer the question. They might say, "I know that our interview time is short, so I prefer to talk about my past teaching than about my family at this point." If an employer doesn't get that message, do you really want to work for him/her?

Do candidates ever say, "I know that's an inappropriate question, and I prefer to not answer"? Yes, I am sure that some candidates have said this. Some may even say, "My training has shown me that is an illegal question, and I prefer to not answer." This is a very confrontational answer, but the person asking is obviously untrained in how to interview if you must go to this degree to point out an illegal question. If this employer pesters you with illegal questions in an interview, what else doesn't she/he know about doing the job? What kind of boss will he/she be?

You are now an adult, and you must decide how you will answer uncomfortable and illegal questions. Interviewing is a two-way street, and you are deciding if you want to work for this district and this administrator, in the interview. Even when an interviewer is not professional, you must be.

Chapter Eight

Preliminary Interviews

When hundreds of applicants apply for one position, personnel directors, secretaries, and administrators sort the paperwork to narrow the pool of candidates. Preliminary interviews are used to further sort candidates. Preliminary interviews can take place by telephone, over the Internet, and at job fairs. No matter the venue of the preliminary interview, the questions asked by phone, over Skype, or at a job fair will probably be quite similar.

Most preliminary interviews are 15 to 30 minutes in length. You are generally asked six to eight questions. The interviewer should have a set list of questions and will be taking notes about your answers. They may have a rubric or evaluation form to rate your answers. If you can see the interviewer, concentrate on your answers, not the evaluation sheet. Do not try to read the evaluation, and do not ask how you did at the end. Asking how you did shows a lack of confidence on your part.

COMMONLY ASKED PRELIMINARY INTERVIEW QUESTIONS

Prepare an answer for each of the following questions. Practice saying your answer to a mirror and/or to another person. While it would be rare to be asked this many questions in a preliminary interview, you should be prepared to answer six to eight questions that are similar to these.

1. Tell us about your preparation to become a teacher.
2. Describe your best teaching experience.
3. Describe a lesson that went well and why it went well.
4. What are the most important curricular topics for this grade/subject level?

5. How have standards guided your teaching (including the Common Core State Standards)?
6. Describe the classroom management and discipline in a classroom where you have taught.
7. What stands out about your teaching experience? Or, what is your greatest strength?
8. Why do you want to teach in our district? What do you know about our community and our students?
9. What have your former supervisors or colleagues said about your teaching?
10. Tell us about your future goals as a teacher.
11. Do you have any questions for me at this point?

Most interviewers wrap up a preliminary interview by stating their hiring timeline and how you will be contacted if you are invited to interview on-site in the district. You should always write down the name of the interviewer or get his/her card if you are meeting in person at a job fair. Thank the interviewer for his/her time.

TELEPHONE INTERVIEWS

A telephone interview may have two calls. The first call is from a staff person who sets up the call, and the second is the actual interview call. Never seem too busy to answer the questions by the staff person, as they too may have input about your hiring. Consider the following advice to prepare for phone interviews.

1. Check your voicemail message. It should be professional in tone.
2. If a secretary or support staff person emails or calls to set up a time for a future phone interview, consider that exchange part of the interview. Be pleasant and strive to be available at the time offered. Secretaries often report back to administrators about the first contact. All email messages should be formal. Use the person's title and write complete sentences. This is not a time to use abbreviations or texting.
3. You should be in a quiet place for the telephone interview. There should be no interruptions or background noise.
4. Your phone should work well. Charge the battery so that you know you have plenty of time, or ask the interviewer to call a landline phone.
5. If family members or roommates could answer your phone, prepare them on how to get you to the phone professionally.

6. Have notes in front of you—on paper or on the laptop. These include notes about your previous work experience, what you know about the district, and questions you may want to ask the interviewer. Some people put a good luck charm on the desk in front of them, too, as their "safe anchor" for a phone interview. Do whatever works for you!

7. Have paper and pen or your laptop so that you can take notes.

8. Write down the name or names of all the people on the call. Use their names if possible, especially when thanking them for the opportunity to talk with them.

9. If you need to ask that someone repeat a question, that's OK, but don't ask for a repeat on most questions. It's a technique to use on a limited basis.

10. Remember to answer questions with PAR and STAR. You want to sell your past preparation, experience, and skills in teaching. (See chapter 7.)

11. While the interviewer cannot see you, he/she can still evaluate your enthusiasm by your tone of voice. As you answer, pretend that you were facing the interviewer, and be animated in your responses.

12. Remember that many employers will eliminate half of the final candidates with a telephone interview. Take the interview seriously.

INTERNET AND JOB FAIR INTERVIEWS

Because technology changes so rapidly, I cannot give details about which Internet systems may be used for your preliminary interview. It might be Skype or a Google program, or another system. If you don't have the technology on your computer, use a computer on your campus. The career center should be able to provide the technology for online interviews.

While the rules for this type of interview are very similar to phone interviews, the technology makes a difference, and the employer can see you. You will want to practice with the technology before the interview, so that you feel confident during the interview. Your appearance and grooming matter. Wear a suit just as you would to a job fair. Look rested and organized.

You will want notes in front of you, and you will want paper and pen or your laptop for taking additional notes. However, don't read notes to answer questions. It's OK to be seen writing. In fact, writing a few notes makes you appear as a serious candidate. Remember to make eye contact. Just as a politician on the campaign trail, you need to work the camera! Smile.

Getting the Most from Job Fairs

There are basically two kinds of job fairs—ones where the recruiters come to college campuses and ones where candidates go to school districts. Both are important. Campus and on-site district job fairs start in the late fall and run through the spring for jobs that start in August. Sometimes there are summer job fairs for high-needs fields like math, science, and special education. Follow these strategies for getting the most from a job fair.

1. Know who will be at the job fair and know what positions are open. Recruiters rarely bother to attend campus job fairs if they don't need teachers, as job fairs cost time and money. Read the advance information about who is attending and what new hires they seek.
2. When attending a district fair, read everything about the fair, the advertised openings, and the district before you attend.
3. If preregistration is required, complete it as stated by the college or district. Some job fairs state that ONLY fully certified people may attend. If you are finishing your program and about to become certified, you do qualify to attend. With the downturn in the economy after 2008, some job seekers began attending teacher job fairs even though they had NO teacher training. Hence, recruiters had to specify that the fairs were for certified personnel.
4. Go to a job fair prepared for a full day. Wear career shoes that are comfortable, as you may be walking all day. If there is no time for a lunch break, carry a granola bar.
5. Don't be intimidated. There may be thousands of people at the fair. As you park your car, you may see many well-dressed, experienced teachers looking for the same jobs that you are. Attend the fair with confidence and be prepared to share your skills, expertise, and experience.

CAREER CLOTHES FOR A JOB FAIR

You really do have to dress for success at a job fair. Your career clothes should be the same as you would wear to a school district for an on-site interview. Consider the following:

1. Both men and women should wear a career suit. Women may choose a suit with a moderate length skirt or tailored slacks. Men should choose a suit and not a pair of khakis with a sport coat.
2. Your clothes and shoes should fit well and be spotlessly clean.
3. Your hair and overall grooming should be neat and clean.
4. While piercings are a very personal matter, remember that most school districts do have teacher dress codes and are conservative in nature. Many candidates choose to remove facial piercings.

Pollock (2011) shared this advice, "When you look great and have impeccable grooming, your confidence improves and you become a more formidable candidate" (p. 57). While the styles of dress and definition of "career clothes" vary by regions within the United States, a dark career suit with a white shirt or blouse is acceptable everywhere. Know the norms for your area and the community where the fair is being held.

Sidebar: A recruiter rated a candidate very low because of attire. Her sundress with a large flower print, and the tiny sweater worn with it, were just not appropriate. She wore high heels, but no pantyhose, and the dress was very tight on her heavy frame. For a woman already almost six feet tall, a dark career suit would have been much more slenderizing. Another recruiter commented, "If that is how she dresses for a job fair and interviews, what would she wear to work on a regular day?"

What to Carry

1. You may carry a small briefcase with your portfolio, extra resumes, paper and pen for note taking, and a laptop.
2. A small leather backpack can be acceptable, but not a worn one that carries your books every day to school.
3. Females should not carry a briefcase and a huge purse. A small purse is acceptable with the briefcase.
4. You will receive material at a job fair—paper applications, DVDs with school information, and sometimes pens, markers, or notepads that advertise the district. Put them in your briefcase or backpack.
5. You may want to carry a granola bar and breath mints. However, do not eat in the interview area. Find a break area.
6. If you carry your cell phone, turn it off. You do not want to be talking with a future employer and take a call. That would end your conversation, the preliminary interview, and your chances for an on-site interview.

What Happens at Job Fairs?

Job fairs vary as the job market varies. When districts need to hire large numbers of new teachers, they advertise their district's salaries and benefits, striving to draw candidates to their table or booth with flashy banners and informative signs. When the market is competitive, districts may attend a college job fair just to gather resumes for the possibility of hiring in late spring or summer.

At many campus job fairs, recruiters talk casually with candidates in the morning and allow a limited number of applicants to have interviews in the afternoon. At other fairs, one person works at a table or booth, answering questions and directing candidates to a second table for quick interviews.

District job fairs generally have tables for every school that is hiring. These tables have administrators and teachers who will talk with job seekers informally and possibly set up some short interviews.

A Job Fair KEY STRATEGY

Every interaction that you have with someone at a job fair can count in your favor or against you. As you enter the building, holding a door might catch the attention of a recruiter who reads your nametag. Later, he or she may remember that you were the one with the nice manners. Offering to carry a box of materials or a poster for a recruiter gets you several extra minutes of one-on-one time with that person. Sell yourself in those two minutes!

At some job fairs, the recruiters take resumes and ask the candidate just one or two questions. These questions might sound pretty basic, "Tell me about your teaching experience" or "Tell me about your teacher preparation." They may or may not be actually listening, so make your answer so interesting that it will grab their attention. In other instances, recruiters will take resumes back to their offices and compare them with the applications that have already been received. If your application is complete and you meet a recruiter at a job fair, making a favorable impression, your application goes into the "under consideration" pile. That's where you want to be.

INDIVIDUAL AND GROUP INTERVIEWS

Some district job fairs have group interviews. A sample group interview might have two to four administrators who are interviewing three to five candidates at once. How intimidating! In this case, an interviewer asks one question, allowing each candidate a few minutes (timed) to answer. If you are interviewed in a situation like this, remember

1. to address the specific interviewer, and to make eye contact with all the interviewers;
2. to listen to others' answers, and then strive to make your answer different;
3. to keep your poise and confidence in check as they are being tested here, and probably rated;
4. to have succinct answers to questions;
5. to be nice to everyone, even the other interviewees. School districts want to hire team players.

FOLLOW-UP FOR JOB FAIRS

There are two things to do after the job fair. First, you should write thank-you notes or emails to the interviewers with whom you met. Next, you should follow up with the districts that were hiring and interested in you. This follow-up might include:

1. Complete an application for the district, if you haven't already.
2. Read the district's web site every few days to watch for postings about new positions.
3. Mail any material to the district that they have requested. This might include a cover letter or letters of recommendation.

FAQS ABOUT PRELIMINARY INTERVIEWS

1. Q: I plan to attend the job fair at my university. Should I try to attend teacher job fairs at other universities?

    A: Yes, if the job fair is open to candidates who are not students at only that campus, you should attend. You may see some of the same district recruiters, but that further reinforces who you are and that you are a committed, persistent candidate.

2. Q: How does the job fair help me to get a job if a district says that they do not know if they are hiring, and it is just February?

    A: The district may be gathering resumes to create a pool of candidates. When an opening does happen, that district may first turn to the candidates its representative met and interviewed at job fairs. A resume collected at a job fair, a positive 15-minute interview, and a completed online application in the district may get you a preliminary phone interview. Yes, there are lots of hurdles to pass before you get an on-site interview.

3. Q: I heard a school counselor say that I shouldn't wear a career suit to a job fair or to an on-site interview. He said that administrators want to know what you will wear every day to work. As a teacher of young children, my wardrobe will include jean skirts, jumpers, and khaki slacks, with lots of colorful vests and sweaters. Can I dress like this for a job fair or on-site interview?

    A: While there will always be disagreement about what to wear, and some administrators don't care if you wear a suit or "teacher clothes," the vast majority of administrators expect career suits at job fairs and interviews.

Chapter Nine

Onsite Interview Questions and Answers

THE ALL-IMPORTANT ONSITE INTERVIEW

An onsite interview is generally earned after a preliminary interview. In some cases, an employer may simply read your resume and decide that he/she wants to invite you to interview. What are the "ground rules" of an onsite interview?

1. Pack your briefcase, or a small backpack, with an extra resume, paper and pencil, possibly a laptop or electronic tablet (iPad), and your portfolio.
2. Wear your best career suit and comfortable walking shoes.
3. Look your best—first impressions matter.
4. If you have been asked to teach a lesson, bring the necessary materials to do so.
5. Practice the drive to the school or district building.
6. Arrive about ten minutes early, and never arrive late.
7. Greet everyone you meet with respect, as any teacher or support staff member may have input into your hiring.
8. Know the name of the person or persons with whom you will be interviewing. Sometimes you meet for an interview with a personnel director and then a building principal. Other times, with a building principal and a department chair or lead teacher. When invited to interview, you should be told whom you will meet. If not, ask.
9. While most teacher interviews are only about an hour, some are longer. Be prepared to stay longer for a school tour or to meet with a group of teachers or other administrators.

10. Do not even take your phone with you into the interview. Leave it in the car.
11. Be very positive and upbeat.
12. Be confident, but not cocky. Assertive, but not aggressive. Be nice. Be polite.

HOW DO INTERVIEWS START?

Interviews start with a handshake, so practice yours before you arrive. Next, you are offered a seat and sometimes offered water, a soft drink, or coffee. Interviews often begin with small talk, as the interviewer might comment about the weather, the drive to the school, or a recent school event. Then comes the inevitable "icebreaker" question. These questions include:

1. Tell me about yourself.
2. What brings you to my office today?
3. What events have brought you to sit in that chair today?
4. Why do you want to be a teacher?

No matter which of these icebreaker questions starts your interview, your answer is almost the same. You want to talk about your preparation, skills, and experience to teach. Remember how your resume has a professional profile that is one to two lines in length? Well, you need a two- to three-line introduction of yourself to break the ice.

Examples:

1. Having just finished a very positive 15-week student teaching experience, I am ready for my first classroom. In student teaching I was able to put all of the strategies and methods that I learned on campus into use, and I can't wait to impact the learning of my own students for a year. Student teaching was too short because I wanted to continue working with the students after I got to know their strengths and personalities.
2. The highlight of my college preparation was my semester abroad in Salamanca, Spain. Living there for five months made me realize the true value of knowing a foreign language. I want to teach Spanish to high school students so that they can study abroad if they choose, and I want to share my experiences with them about living in another culture. It all starts with that first foreign language class and simply learning to say, "Hola, cómo estás?"
3. Having worked in the business world for nine years, I can teach my students about real world experiences. I can convince students that

how they speak and how they write will help them to become employed and to stay employed. I made sophomore English very practical in my internship, and I can make it come alive for all high school students.

Once the icebreaker question is over, the "nuts and bolts" questions begin. Remember that administrators want to know if you know how to teach so that students achieve success. They want to know if you can organize a classroom and manage student behavior. By explaining past successes with specific teaching scenarios, you will convince them that you can achieve success as a teacher in a future classroom. Past behavior is the best predictor of future performance.

PREPARING TO ANSWER ONSITE INTERVIEW QUESTIONS

As stated earlier, you must prepare for general questions for a preliminary interview. These questions are built on curriculum, planning, management, differentiation of instruction, raising student achievement, assessment, and professionalism. When you get an onsite interview, be prepared to answer some general questions again. These questions are similar to those for a preliminary interview, but may be asked slightly differently.

For the following questions, write out a few key phrases of your answer. A starting point for answering each question is included. For each question, you will see a brief suggestion for answering the question immediately before it.

1. Q: Tell about a lesson that went well (or badly) and why it went well (or badly).

   A: Emphasize what you did and what you will or will not do again.
2. Q: Describe a classroom management plan that you have used successfully.

   A: Show a plan from your portfolio with rules, positives, and corrective actions/consequences.
3. Q: Tell about your lesson planning. Where do you start in planning a lesson and what steps are included in a lesson?

   A: Show a plan and talk about a warm-up, presenting new material, student practice, and informal assessment.
4. Q: Describe the physical classroom where you have worked and routines and procedures for that classroom.

   A: Describe how students enter the room and get settled.
5. Q: Describe student achievement in a classroom where you have worked.

A: Talk about raising student achievement, even if just for one student.

6. Q: Describe assessment and grading in a classroom where you have worked.

A: Show a grading scale or plan. Talk about formative vs. summative assessment.

7. Q: How have you used student data to inform lesson planning and assessment?

A: Talk about students' preknowledge and how it is used to plan a lesson. Pre- and post-tests can be discussed to answer this question.

8. Q: How have you differentiated instruction to meet the needs of students?

A: Remediation can be discussed, as well as challenging gifted learners.

GRADE AND SUBJECT LEVEL-SPECIFIC QUESTIONS

During an onsite interview, expect very specific questions, especially if the interviewer knows the exact position opening, such as a high school math teacher for algebra and geometry. For elementary positions, you may be asked questions about different grade levels, as you are being hired to work for a district, not necessarily a specific grade in one school. Some districts may require interviews for substitute teaching positions, as well, especially if the position is long term.

Questions for a Substitute Teaching Position

1. Q: Describe your experience working with children.

A: If you are a fully certified teacher, describe student teaching or past jobs. If not, consider work with daycare, scouts, or sports teams that you have completed.

2. Q: Tell about your availability to work. Are you available on days when called or do you need advance notice?

A: Be honest in your response. The best substitutes report that they are prepared to leave the house early every day, so that if a call comes in on that day, they can leave.

3. Q: Describe classroom organization and management techniques that can be used when you are a substitute teacher.

A: Substitutes should get to know students' names, should read the school's policies, and should be aware of an individual teacher's plan. (See, for example, Wong and Wong, 2009.)

4. Q: How have you communicated with teachers in the past about their classes?

A: Substitutes should write a detailed report at the end of the day for the teacher.

5. Q: What materials or time-filling activities have you used when no plans are left by the teacher?

A: Describe a "teaching bag" of activities, such as books to read to elementary students, word puzzles, number games, and DVDs to show.

Questions for a Preschool Position

1. Q: Explain how preschool is different from day care.

A: Explain as if you were talking to a parent. You may want to start your answer by saying that if the interviewer were the parent, this is what you would have said.

2. Q: Describe a procedure or routine that you have used to get a three- or four-year-old into the classroom and settled.

A: Your answer may include past experiences with getting children to "let go" of parents and how you have handled that issue.

3. Q: What are some developmentally appropriate lessons and activities that you have taught? Why were they appropriate in meeting the needs of children this age?

A: Be specific in describing one or two items and addressing the "why" part of the question.

4. Q: How have you introduced prereading or reading skills with this age group?

A: Describe word or sound activities that you have used.

Questions for Kindergarten, First, and Second Grade Positions

1. Q: Describe your approach to teaching reading.

A: Talk about methods and/or programs that you have used.

2. Q: Describe specific math topics that you have taught.

A: Be specific about the topics, and you may include a name of a series or textbook that you have used.

3. Q: How do you accurately assess student learning without formal grades with young students?

A: Talk about checklists of items that students have mastered or authentic assessments where you write about student progress with narratives.

Questions for Upper Elementary Grade Positions

1. Q: Tell about your experiences preparing students for standardized tests.

   A: Talk about reviewing and helping students with stress management.

2. Q: How have you taught reading to students of this age?

   A: Explain a balanced approach and/or specific strategies and programs you have used.

3. Q: How have you integrated subjects for students?

   A: Discuss integrating social studies or science into reading or math lessons.

4. Q: What are some developmentally appropriate activities that students this age really enjoy?

   A: Talk about past lessons that you taught that students enjoyed.

Questions for Middle School Positions

1. Q: How have you taught reading directly, or how have you taught reading by integrating it into another subject?

   A: Be ready to share specifics of how every teacher is a reading teacher when working in a middle school.

2. Q: Describe the developmental needs of middle school students.

   A: Be specific about an individual student or a class with whom you have worked.

3. Q: Much has been written about team teaching and about teaching teams in middle schools. Describe your experience with either of these or with collaboration of middle school teachers.

   A: If you have experienced this, talk about it. If not, talk about collaborating with your assigned cooperating teacher during the student teaching experience.

4. Q: How have you helped prepare middle school students for high school? Or, how have you motivated a middle school student whose work was weak?

   A: Talk about how you motivate all students and about teaching students the study skills that they will need to succeed in high school. If you have supervised a class trip to the high school, talk about that, or a similar experience.

Questions for General High School Positions

1. Q: How have you motivated students to achieve in your class?

   A: Talk about engaging activities and lessons taught.

2. Q: How have you encouraged students to stay in school and graduate?

   A: Describe any activity that you have conducted or any strategies you learned during student teaching about motivating students to graduate.

3. Q: How have you prepared students for standardized tests, end-of-course tests, or graduation tests?

   A: Share examples of what you have done or have seen done in a school.

4. Q: How have you used homework in a high school setting?

   A: Share a specific example, preferably with a visual from your portfolio.

5. Q: Tell about classroom management for a typical high school classroom. What has worked for you?

   A: Answer with the example of a classroom management plan from your portfolio. Talk about routines and procedures, even for 17-year-olds.

Questions for English/Language Arts Positions

1. Q: How have you implemented the Common Core State Standards?

   A: Show a lesson plan or curriculum map with the standard as a focus.

2. Q: What topics have you had the most experience with for this grade?

   A: Talk about your experience with writing, literature, grammar, and the like.

3. Q: How have you used a high school English class to improve students' reading skills?

   A: Specific examples are best. Share about vocabulary, comprehension, and other topics.

4. Q: How have you dealt with a diversity of reading levels in one class?

   A: Answer by talking about a lesson with differentiation.

5. Q: Describe your favorite lesson for this grade/subject.

   A: Show a lesson plan and describe it.

Questions for Mathematics Positions

1. Q: How have you implemented the Common Core State Standards?

   A: Show a lesson plan or curriculum map with a standard as a focus.

2. Q: Describe your experience with a favorite math topic that you like to teach.

   A: Describe a specific lesson plan, and show it from your portfolio.

3. Q: How have you assessed students' previous knowledge so that you are not teaching what they already know, but are also not teaching above their knowledge level?

    A: Talk about informal vs. formal assessments, interest inventories, and ungraded pretests.

4. Q: How have you dealt with math homework in the past?

    A: Describe or show a homework policy or assignment that you have used.

5. Q: What were the standardized test scores like in your previous teaching experience?

    A: A picture is worth a thousand words. Show some results, with all identifying information removed. Remember that student teaching is teaching experience.

Questions for Science Positions

1. Q: Tell about the standards for your area of science.

    A: Discuss a lesson that you taught that was built on a specific standard.

2. Q: How was science tested at your previous school of employment (or student teaching)?

    A: Show a sample test you created, or discuss end-of-course testing.

3. Q: Tell about the use of labs in your previous school.

    A: Describe what was available and how the lab was integrated into the class.

4. Q: How have you motivated/encouraged students to take advanced science classes?

    A: Talk about the jobs available if students are "science literate" and if they major in science in college.

Questions for Social Studies/History Positions

1. Q: Tell about the standards for your area of social science and how you have incorporated those standards into past lessons.

    A: Describe a lesson plan with a standard, or show a curriculum map with the standards listed for a unit.

2. Q: Besides lecturing students, which strategies have you used to teach in your field?

    A: Talk about the value of discussions, role-plays, debates, web searches, and other methods.

3. Q: What is a current trend or controversy in the field of social studies or history? How have you dealt with this trend or controversy?

A: Answers may vary widely for your state or region. Some of the debates center on how much social studies/history should be taught, as high school curricula center on English, math, and science. There is often debate about which eras of history deserve the most time in the curriculum.

Questions for Foreign Languages Positions

1. Q: Much has been written about total immersion in a foreign language classroom. About how much of a class that you have taught would have been in the target foreign language? Why?

   A: Answers vary, but most agree that a foreign language teacher should use as much of the target language as possible.

2. Q: Describe your experience teaching speaking, grammar, or culture.

   A: Tell about a very successful lesson, perhaps one that incorporated all of the above.

3. Q: How have your former students used the language outside of the classroom? Or, how have you hosted a foreign language dinner or play so that students could use the language outside of their classroom?

   A: Describe an event that you participated in as a student, or one you helped with as a student teacher.

Questions for Arts Positions

1. Q: Describe a typical lesson that you have taught that involved students making something.

   A: Show a picture from your portfolio to support this answer.

2. Q: How have you graded students in the art classroom? Or, how have you set up a grading scale for art?

   A: Provide information about formative and summative grading or informal vs. formal.

3. Q: How have you motivated students who feel that they are weak in art?

   A: If you provide a specific student example, don't use a proper name.

4. Q: What special routines and procedures have you put in place for the management of an art classroom?

   A: Talk about safety issues and/or cleaning up.

Questions for Music Positions

1. Q: Describe a typical class practice that went well and why it went well.

   A: Talk about your organization of that practice session.

2. Q: Describe a concert or marching band event that went well and why it went well.

   A: Describe the organization that led up to the event that made it go smoothly.

3. Q: How have you used the parents, PTO, PTA, or other band boosters to help support the music program?

   A: Talk about an example from student teaching or from when you were in high school that you would like to repeat as a teacher.

4. Q: What have been special management issues that you have dealt with in leading a chorus or band?

   A: One answer to this might be to talk about dealing with large student numbers.

Questions for Health/Physical Education Positions

1. Q: Getting all students dressed and participating is always an issue in physical education. How have you dealt with these issues?

   A: Describe successful ideas from student teaching or your previous job.

2. Q: How have you encouraged students who are not in shape to succeed in physical activities?

   A: Talk about differentiating instruction so that students can gain strength and get in shape in reasonable ways.

3. Q: How have you encouraged good sportsmanship in your previous classes?

   A: Give a specific example about having students shake hands and the like.

4. Q: How have you addressed adolescent obesity in your health and/or physical education classes?

   A: Describe a lesson about healthy lifestyles.

Questions for Special Education for All Grade Levels Positions

1. Q: Describe your past experience with exceptional learners. Be specific.

   A: In most cases, the employer will ask about a certain population, such as students with autism, ADD, or learning disabilities.

2. Q: Which strategies have been most effective in your work with students with _____ ?

   A: Employers are looking for answers that demonstrate your preparation and experience with these students.

3. Q: Tell us about your work with total inclusion (or mainstreaming, or pull-out programs).

   A: Employers are seeking to find out your experience with students in a specific special education setting.

4. Q: Describe your work with one student's Individualized Education Plan (IEP).

   A: Answer with a specific student's issues, but do not use an actual name.

5. Q: Describe your work with Response to Intervention (RTI).

   A: Talk about what you learned, even if you were an observer in the process at this point in your career.

6. Q: Tell about a parent conference regarding a student with an exceptionality.

   A: Many new teachers have not conducted these conferences, due to confidentiality issues, but you can talk about observing a conference, or about the preparation that must be done to prepare for a conference.

7. Q: Tell about your work collaborating with other teachers.

   A: Collaboration and being a "team player" is especially important in the field of special education. Have a vignette ready to tell.

HOW TO ANSWER "BAD" QUESTIONS

Many administrators who interview and hire new teachers have never had any training in how to do so. They tend to interview as they were interviewed, starting with the timeless question, "tell me about yourself," and ending with "where do you see yourself in five to ten years?" If you are interviewed by someone who asks vague questions, consider answering with behavior-based answers anyway. In other words, no matter how the interviewer phrases the questions, you can talk about your teacher preparation, your experience, and your expertise. For example, when asked, "tell me about yourself," your answer should begin with your professional profile—a couple of strong lines that summarize your preparation and experience.

If you are asked about your biggest weakness, phrase your answer to be positive. For example, "My biggest weakness is that I won't give up on a student, especially one who may be close to getting lost in the school system." If an interviewer comments that this isn't a weakness, you can reply that you are there to share your most positive attributes.

Another question that occasionally comes up in interviews is to ask the candidate how his/her colleagues or professors would describe them. Again, be positive about yourself without sounding like a braggart. Interviews are the time to highlight your work.

KEY: While you are trying to sell yourself in an interview, do not be aggressive. An overly assertive candidate is not viewed well. Do not talk about past negative situations. A candidate who says how awful the teachers were at a previous school is perceived as a person who will be negative about his/her new colleagues.

TEACHING A LESSON AS PART OF AN ONSITE INTERVIEW

It is becoming more common for a candidate to teach a sample lesson to a group of students as part of the job interview. This is never done without informing the candidate. If asked to teach a model lesson, find out as much as possible about the students, and the curriculum. If you are to teach a lesson that fits with the students' textbook, you should be sent that information ahead of time so that you can prepare.

One hint for teaching a class is to begin with a quick activity to know names. Bring a set of index cards and have the students print their names on the cards, then fold them and place on their desks so that you know each student's name. This just helps you to get established.

Again, you may be asked to teach a lesson about a specific topic tied to the students' text or curriculum, or you may be asked to teach a topic that is one of your favorites. Sometimes a candidate is asked to teach the lesson to the other teachers, not the students. Have fun with the lesson. Appearing confident is a big part of acing this type of interview.

BE PREPARED TO ASK QUESTIONS

The majority of interviewers ask if you have questions for them. What should you ask?

1. You may ask a follow-up question to something you have read on their web site that hasn't been discussed in the interview. Example, "Your district web site mentioned the 2010 award for staff development. What did that award mean for your district?"
2. It is always good to ask about the professional development offered to teachers, if that has not been discussed by the employer. Examples: Describe the orientation and new teacher induction offered in this district.
3. What ongoing professional development is offered to all teachers?

4. The employer should discuss salaries and benefits. Often, the interviewer simply hands the candidate this information in written form, or refers them back to the district web site. If the employer has not discussed this, you may ask, "Is the salary and benefit information posted online current?" If nothing is posted (very rare), then you may ask how that information will be provided to you as a candidate. Be diplomatic here. Do your homework and know the district web site thoroughly before asking any salary and benefit questions.

5. If the employer has not provided a timeline for hiring, you may ask about the timeline. Phrase your question diplomatically, "What is your timeline for hiring, and when may I expect to hear back from the district?"

FAQS ABOUT INTERVIEWS

1. If I am asked to stay longer than an hour, perhaps to sit in on a faculty meeting or to meet a group of teachers over a lunch, should I stay?

    YES, absolutely. You should always stay when invited to do so, as this indicates your true interest in the district and its teachers.

2. If I know a teacher or teachers in this district, should I mention their names?

    The answer to this depends on how you know them. If you know some teachers from your previous substitute teaching or field experience, you can say this, and then say something positive about their comments regarding teaching in the district. If asked why you want to work in the district, you can say that some of your acquaintances/friends have reported excellent experiences about their positions, and they encouraged you to apply here.

3. If I know an administrator or school board member in this district, should I bring up their names?

    Not necessarily. If you know an administrator or school board member well, you might be better served by using them as a reference in your application paperwork, not by trying to "name-drop" in an interview. Also, using someone's name in the interview might work against you, as hiring someone because of connections is viewed very negatively by some employers. It is best to talk about your preparation and experience.

4. Should I leave an electronic portfolio or copies of lessons and units with the interviewer?

    There is no one right answer to this question. If you do choose to leave a flash drive with your electronic portfolio, or a card with directions to your web site, be prepared that some interviewers will not go to their computer and look at it. If you do leave materials, do not expect them back. Leave a short, clearly written portfolio, if it is on paper or electronic. If you have online materials, it is better to list them on your resume, as some interviewers may look at these materials when considering you for a final interview.

5. Should I tell the interviewer that I am a finalist at another district?

Be an adult when interviewing, and do not release too much personal information. The interviewer is not your guidance counselor or in the business to give you parental advice. I would not give out this information. If asked if you are under consideration elsewhere, your answer should be very diplomatic. "In these economic times, I have applied for multiple positions. I will consider offers as they are made, and I plan to be a teacher with my own classroom for the upcoming school year. Again, I am interested in your district because . . ." It is up to you how you answer.

6. I have heard that minority candidates and those with multiple certifications in high needs fields may be recruited forcefully to commit at the end of an interview. Should I commit to a job in an interview?

Any strong candidate may be offered a letter of intent, which is similar to a contract, during an interview. If this happens, you should wonder why the district is in such a rush to fill the position. If offered, it is generally best to say, "Thank you for this offer, and it sounds excellent to me. I would like to know your timeline for my response." Do not say that you need to talk to family, parents, or even a job counselor before accepting, as this indicates that you do not make your own decisions. Most employers would give a minimum of three days as a timeline to hear your decision.

7. If asked if I have reservations about working in the district, should I actually state those concerns to the interviewer?

It probably depends on the nature of the concerns. If you have heard that the teachers there are not supported by a certain principal, you should not reveal that type of information in an answer. If your concern is large class size, a building undergoing remodeling, or something like that, it is OK to ask about the possibility of reduction of class size in the future or the timetable for getting a classroom that has been finished.

Chapter Ten

After the Interview

What is expected after the on-site interview? Are there things that can be done to help one's case to get the job?

THE VALUE OF THANK-YOU NOTES

Thank-you notes are still expected by employers after an interview. A note may be written and sent through email or on paper. Guidelines for email thank-you notes include:

1. Write the email as if it were a formal note.
2. Have a salutation, such as Dr. John Smith or Ms. Pamela Smith.
3. Use complete sentences, not phrases, and do not use abbreviations or shortened words as one might in a text message or tweet.
4. Say something about your continued interest in the position, in addition to thanking the interviewers for their time.
5. Add something you learned about the school or district that you didn't know earlier.
6. End the email message with a formal "Sincerely" and your name.

If you send a paper thank-you note, it may be typed or handwritten. You should edit it and check it very carefully for spelling, punctuation, and grammar. Remember that your handwriting is being evaluated in the note. Your handwriting should be clear and easy to read. Legibility matters. Samples follow:

Sample 1

Mr. Carl Waters:

I would like to thank you for the interview on Monday the 7th. I especially enjoyed getting to see the third grade wing and getting to observe in Mrs. Pratt's class for a few minutes. While I was aware of your school's past Blue Ribbon awards, I didn't know about the "family learning environment" until I saw it for myself. I can see how much students can achieve in this environment, and I want to work in a school with this approach, as it matches my own experience helping students to learn.

Thank you for your consideration, and I look forward to hearing from you.

Sincerely,

Amy Thomas

Sample 2

Mrs. Nina Rouan:

I would like to thank you for meeting with me yesterday. I appreciated getting to spend two hours with you and your faculty and having the chance to talk with two teachers from the math department. Working at a middle school that is growing at the rate of 70 students a year would be a great experience for me, as I would have the chance to teach a variety of courses. The students' energy levels were high and both students and faculty seemed highly engaged.

Again, thank you for your consideration and I am now more interested than ever in a position at Carsen Middle School. I would love to be a Carsen Cougar!

Sincerely,

Abby Young

HOW TO FOLLOW-UP ABOUT OFFERS

After the thank-you notes are sent, how long does a candidate wait to hear back about an offer? The timeline varies widely, as some districts must complete considerable paperwork and contact several offices before making an offer. When the job market is a tight one, an employer may take advantage of this and interview at least three to five people on-site before making an offer. Sometimes an employer makes an offer, waits several days to hear back from the top candidate, and then contacts the other candidates. So, it is usually at least a week before a candidate hears about an offer, or hears that he/she was not hired. Many districts call all candidates to inform them that they have not been hired. Some send a letter to those who are not offered jobs. In a few cases, districts fail to get back to candidates who are not offered jobs.

Employers should explain their hiring timeline and how candidates are contacted during the interview. If not, ask about those issues. Do not be surprised if a secretary or administrative assistant calls, and not the employer with whom you interviewed. Every district has a different policy.

When contacted with a job offer, it is certainly OK to be excited. You may say yes to the offer when it is made, if all the questions you had about the job were answered in the interview or in follow-up communications. In fact, building principals want candidates to be excited about a job offer. Many want to hear the yes response immediately.

It is also acceptable to be gracious about the offer, but to let the employer know that you still need a little time to consider it. Two to three days is a reasonable time to think about an offer. It is not a good idea to ask for more time after that, or to tell a potential employer that you are waiting on a different offer from another district. Many employers simply do not like being told that you are hesitating and will want an answer immediately. Be an adult. Make your decisions. If you interview on-site in a district, be prepared to say yes or no to an offer when contacted.

What happens after the initial offer is made? A job offer is usually considered to be "informal" until you receive a letter of intent or a contract. Contracts are not usually formalized until after the board of education meetings. As a reminder, you work for a school district, not an individual school, and the board of education is your employer. Contracts are formal documents and state how many days you have to sign and return them.

A letter of intent is the district's intent to employ you if the board approves your hiring. If you are asked to sign a letter of intent, it represents your statement that if offered the position, you will accept. Letters of intent are often used in large districts that need to ensure they are getting sufficient numbers of new hires to fill all positions. The letters serve to keep strong candidates from accepting jobs elsewhere while waiting for a school board to issue formal contracts.

Do candidates say yes verbally and then say no when the contract arrives? Yes, some candidates do this, although it is not considered to be good professional practice. School district administrators know each other and talk frequently about everything, including personnel. School districts need a full faculty when the doors open for every new school year, and they count on new hires being honest in their commitments.

What happens to candidates who sign a contract and then find another job? Technically, a school district can sue a candidate for breach of contract, but they rarely do so, because it is easier to hire someone else and avoid the legal fees. Besides, who wants a teacher who was ordered by the court to report for work? Not fulfilling a contract should be considered a very serious act. Not fulfilling a contract means that you will never be considered for another job in that district, or perhaps not even in that area or state. A district would certainly report your default to its state board of education and your teaching credentials could be at stake. The few people that I know who defaulted on signed contracts did so to accept higher paying jobs in the business world and therefore never intended to teach at any time in the future. That is a really big decision to make, and one never knows how far that decision may reach to work against them in the future.

FAQS ABOUT TEACHING JOB OFFERS

1. Q: I know a person who interviewed for a high school teaching position and was told during the interview that she would be teaching five college prep science courses. When she arrived for new teacher orientation, she discovered that her assignment was five general science classes with the lowest achieving students in the school. She immediately discussed this with her employer and was told that "you were hired to teach science for the district and no specific assignments are guaranteed." How did this happen?

   A: Sometimes employers say what they think the assignment will be, but staffing issues change the final outcome of the assignments. Perhaps a veteran teacher requested a change, and seniority guidelines forced the change. Perhaps the interviewer did not really know the assignments and his/her best guess was the college-bound courses. It is unfortunate that the candidate was led to believe one thing and that it did not happen, but it is true that a teacher works for a district, and assignments can change at any time before the school year begins, or even during a school year. Teachers need to be aware of seniority guidelines, as well as teacher contract/union agreements, as these agreements often dictate assignments.

2. Q: I have an endorsement on my teaching certificate for the teaching of English as a Second Language, as it was required from the university where I graduated. I do not want to teach in a classroom working with English language learners, however. I do not list my endorsement on my resume, and I will not discuss it in interviews. If hired for a job, a district will see my endorsement on my paperwork. Can the district still place me in a classroom for ESL and not honor my request to work in a regular classroom?

A: Yes, the district can request that you work in any classroom where you have the appropriate certification or endorsement. Refusing to work in a classroom where you are placed means that the district can release you at any time. Many education students do earn enough extra hours in English as a second language or in special education for additional endorsements to certification. This makes students more employable as young teachers but may mean for some challenging work, too.

3. Q: I have worked for three summers at a great job at a national park. By working the full summer, I get an excellent bonus. As I approach my first full-time teaching job, I realize that my summer job ends four days after the job at the school district is scheduled to start. How flexible are districts about start dates and should I negotiate this date before accepting the job?

A: School districts are NOT flexible about start dates, and even suggesting this issue during an interview will most likely cause you to lose the offer. If you accept the job, and then try to negotiate arriving several days late, you are in breach of contract and have started out with a big negative for your first evaluation. Your new colleagues will not be receptive, either. First impressions matter tremendously, and you need to be at the new job rested and ready to work.

4. Q: I have heard that if one is a finalist and is not offered a position, that asking why is a good idea. Should I ask an employer for their suggestions about what I should do differently next time?

A: These are two very different questions. School districts are not supposed to release any information about reasons for hiring or not hiring anyone. If you ask the first question, a well-trained employer should say that he/she cannot discuss these issues. If an interviewer tells you a reason that you were not hired, he/she can get into trouble with the school district, as this is confidential information.

Asking for advice or suggestions on how to interview is a different question. However, a well-trained employer will not answer this question, either. Some interviewers do answer the question, but are very vague in their answers, responding with "prepare a few better answers to questions about student achievement," or "strive to show a little more confidence."

It is best NOT to ask any questions about why you were not hired or about what to do next time. It is much better to turn to your college career center for more preparation or practice interviews.

5. Q: After being turned down for a job, a teacher from that school told me that the principal hired her friend's son for the position. The teacher told me that the principal had made up her mind before she interviewed anyone that she was going to hire the friend's son, but she still interviewed four people. Is this legal?

    A: Yes, nothing illegal was done here. The friend's son may have been the very best candidate, and the principal may have known this from the start. However, it could have also just been a case of "cronyism." Some employers are adamant about hiring only teachers who are people that they know, or who know people that they know. Quite frankly, you don't want to work in that environment anyway.

TRACKING YOUR INTERVIEWS

In today's job market, a teacher job candidate can expect to apply for many positions before receiving the first preliminary interview. It may take several preliminary interviews to win the all-important on-site interview, and it may take several on-site interviews before getting a job offer. Persistence matters.

After each interview, write down the names of the people with whom you met. Keep their business cards. Consider a paper file or an electronic one with all the information you learned in the interview.

Write down as many of the interview questions as you remember. Next, write down phrases or ideas for what you might have said differently. Practice answers to the questions that you were asked, as you will probably be asked that question again by another interviewer.

One teacher said that she had interviewed for five different positions when an employer called. She was on the phone trying to remember the specifics of that job as she spoke with the potential employer, as the interview had been several weeks ago. It was a follow-up call to ask about her interest in the position, but not a job offer. After the phone conversation, she wished she had a file or notebook or her iPad with notes in front of her. With the notes in front of her, she could have had a better conversation with the potential employer.

It is important to continue job searching full-time as the new school year opens. When classes are in session, a district has immediate needs for positions. August, September, and October openings have to be filled quickly, and districts tend to turn to their files of strong candidates to find a teacher.

NETWORKING

It can be very helpful to create a network of friends and teachers for support during the job search process. Consider keeping in touch with all of the education students in your last college classes. Create an online conversation with those who student taught the semester that you did. Use Facebook to read comments from teacher education job seekers from around the country (or the world). Consider the following two sites on Facebook:

www.teachers-teachers.com
www.schoolspring.com

While it may be tempting to post a horror story from one of your own interviews, remember that what you post is going public. It is not advised that you post a message about an "idiot" who interviewed you, or about how awful a school district appeared when you toured it.

It can be very disheartening to interview with a district at two or three job fairs, and then to interview again in the district, only to be told that you will not be extended an offer. Consider these interviews learning experiences, even if painful. The one certainty is that you won't get hired if you don't interview.

Chapter Eleven

Your First Year of Teaching

WHEN HIRED

It is a great feeling to get your first teaching job. Celebrate! Then start getting reading for the first day of school. Consider the following steps as a count-down to your first day of school:

1. Complete all paperwork needed by the district—contract, criminal background check, physical exam, insurance, and tax forms.
2. If you live within commuting distance to your school, practice your commute at the regular time so that you know how much time is needed. Being late for orientation or the first day is not a good thing.
3. If you need to move to the new district, allow time to get settled into your apartment before school starts.
4. Organize your career wardrobe. Learn about the dress code or the dress "norms" and follow them. It is always better to overdress at first than to be reminded by the new employer that you are not appropriate-ly dressed.
5. Find out how early you can work in your room. Count the desks and see if enough are in the room for the rosters you are given.
6. Ask where supplies are kept and see what is available. Are you pro-vided with paper, pens, bulletin board supplies, and the like?
7. Gather the supplies at back-to-school sales.
8. Work in your room to make bulletin boards and to organize desks for a walking pattern that gets students in and out quickly. However, make sure that once you work in your room, it can be locked and secured. One new teacher worked a whole week in her room, only to return to school for orientation to find that people had taken her bulletin board

materials and learning centers because they thought they were left from the previous year and were "up for grabs."
9. Find out where student books are kept and get class sets for your room.
10. Get to know the teachers near your room, as they may be invaluable in answering questions the first week of class.

NEW TEACHER ORIENTATION

Your evaluation for re-employment does not begin with your first classroom visit from the principal. Your participation in new teacher orientation is also your first evaluation. Your administrators will note if you are on time, if you sit in the front or back, and if you participate. First impressions matter. Sit up front and take notes. Do not get your cell phone out at any time. Do not text or look bored. If you ask questions, make sure that they are pertinent ones.

Use orientation time to start making collegial friends. Be pleasant. Principals often ask veteran teachers for their input on "the new hire" when it comes time to determine next year's contracts. What you do in new teacher evaluation will be remembered all year. Consider these sessions to be VERY important. Do not complain. Schools have enough negative teachers already.

New teacher orientation should include:

1. Explanation of the school's curriculum
2. Explanation of the school's classroom management and discipline plan
3. School safety laws and guidelines (fire, tornado, violence prevention)
4. Grading policies
5. Updates on state laws that affect teachers
6. A school calendar that includes dates for state testing
7. Description of how new teachers are evaluated for retention and tenure
8. How to apply for grants and/or professional development
9. Important information about school demographics and funding
10. Guidelines for parent communication and parent open houses
11. The school or district's mentor program guidelines
12. Information about upcoming new teacher seminars/workshops
13. What's available from the school/district for technology
14. Which offices provide which services to teachers (payroll, medical, etc.)
15. Some get-acquainted activities or a bus tour of the district

MENTOR PROGRAMS

Some states mandate that all new hires must be provided with a mentor for at least their first year of teaching. Other states do not have this requirement, but districts may provide mentors for their new teachers with their own programs. What does a mentor do for a new teacher and how can you get the most out of being paired with a veteran teacher who serves as your mentor? (See, for example, Clement and Wilkins, 2011.)

A mentor's roles can vary widely. If you are assigned a mentor, the first thing to find out is his/her role in your work. Does the mentor have any evaluative duties? Will he/she report on your progress to your lead teacher, department chair, or principal? Or is her/his role nonevaluative and supportive in nature? Knowing the role of the mentor is critically important.

Once the role is known, find out how the mentor can help. Common mentor roles include:

1. Helping the new teacher to set up the classroom
2. Assisting in finding books, materials, and supplies
3. Collaborating with the new teacher to write a classroom management plan
4. Explaining all school policies
5. Observing in the new teacher's classroom to suggest ideas for management or teaching
6. Inviting the new teacher to observe in the mentor's classroom
7. Attending a professional conference together
8. Reading lesson plans and talking about all aspects of teaching
9. Answering questions
10. Sharing materials and resources
11. Discussing parent communications and conferences
12. Assisting with the school's online grading program and other technology

The mentor is *not* a teacher's assistant or paraprofessional. The new teacher should not ask a mentor to make photocopies or to simply give him/her old tests or worksheets. New teachers should remember that their assigned mentors are also full-time teachers, and that they are very busy with their own students. A mentor can be considered to be a professional colleague who shares past experiences and provides help as needed. Ask the mentor questions and use his/her expertise to think through your own plans and projects. The mentor should have received training for his/her role, but some mentors are simply assigned and may tell you that they don't have any idea what they are supposed to do. In that case, discuss what they might do before the school year begins. Many first-year teachers consider mentors to be just like first aid—a quick and temporary assistance when needed. Others consider their mentor to be their lifesaver and feel that they might not survive their first year of teaching without that supporter.

If you are not assigned a formal mentor, it is a good idea to get to know your colleagues well and to establish a support network of your own. You might find a teacher is an expert in managing a classroom, and ask if you can observe his/her room for an hour. Another teacher might be willing to let you observe how she teaches specific lessons. Asking advice shows that you are willing to learn. Don't become a pest or try to get others to do your work, but do reach out to others and listen to their stories of teaching.

TAKING ADVANTAGE OF OTHER PROFESSIONAL DEVELOPMENT OPPORTUNITIES

Some districts provide new teacher workshops that are scheduled throughout the year. Whether these seminars are required or not, try to attend them all. Topics for new teacher workshops are designed around the needs of new hires and are generally aligned with the school year. For example, seminars that are offered once a month might include the following topics:

1. Getting started with the new school year
2. Classroom management that works
3. Communicating with parents—calls, emails, letters, and conferences
4. Working with students with exceptionalities
5. Working with students before and after the major holidays and breaks
6. Stress management for you
7. Teaching strategies to keep students engaged until the end of the school year
8. Differentiation of instruction
9. What you need to know about standardized testing
10. Ending the school year on a positive note

Some school districts may offer seminars and require that you attend a certain number of the total number available. Other districts may offer these topics as online seminars with chat groups for the new teachers. Online new teacher induction is growing rapidly. A district may offer a combination of seminars and online training, requiring the new hires to complete a certain number of each as a stipulation for re-hiring. Required or not, your attendance at these events will most likely be considered when the decision to renew your contract for a second year is made.

CHECKLIST FOR THE FIRST DAY OF SCHOOL

While one may never feel completely ready for the first day of student attendance, having a checklist provides a starting point for feeling organized. Consider the following when preparing for the first day of student attendance.

1. Know which students to expect. Have desks for them and have one or two extras because first-day rosters often change.
2. Have some decorations in your room, such as a welcome bulletin board.
3. Post your name and the name of the class on your door and inside the room.
4. Have a system for getting the students into the room and seated quickly. For young students, have names on desks. For older students have a seating chart on the screen or hand out cards with row numbers and seat numbers.
5. Have something posted on the screen, board, or poster for students to do immediately upon entering the room. This may be a get-acquainted activity or a short interest inventory.
6. Spend time the first day introducing yourself and having students learn each other's names.
7. Use the first few days of school to teach routines and procedures as well as your classroom management plan—even with high school students.
8. Have your management plan posted on the wall. This plan should have rules, supportive feedback, and corrective actions. (See, for example, Canter, 2010.)
9. Know one teacher down the hall well enough to ask him/her questions.
10. Know where the student restrooms are located. Students will ask you!
11. Get to know the custodian and the school secretary/administrative assistant and what they can and cannot do for you. These people are usually lifesavers for new teachers.
12. Consider having tissues, band-aids, hand lotion, hand sanitizer, and other items in the room for student use. This way, students shouldn't ask to leave the room for these items.
13. Lock your purse in a desk drawer or file cabinet. Don't carry much money or any valuables to work. Student theft is rampant.
14. Have a mini-lesson ready so that students realize you are going to be teaching and that they are going to be learning every day.

15. Check your email or your school mailbox before students arrive on the first day of school. There may be last minute announcements from the administration.
16. Provide students with a letter to take home about your class. For young students this is an introduction to you, classroom management, and to the curriculum. For older students, this may be a syllabus.
17. Teach your routine for ending class, or for ending the day.
18. Make sure you know how young children leave the building and catch the bus or meet their parents.
19. Take notes on what went well and what you need to re-do on day two. Get in the habit of writing notes on your daily plans so that you have better plans the second year.
20. Do something positive for yourself, like taking a walk or going to the gym. Get some sleep and be ready for day two.

Throughout the First Year

The first year of teaching is a learning experience, even though you have completed hours of coursework and student teaching. Unlike some other professions, where a new hire is not given many responsibilities immediately, new teachers are expected to run their classrooms and to cover the mandated curriculum just like a veteran teacher. You are the "real" teacher from the first day.

There is no such thing as being too organized. Keep files for each class and for the units that you teach. Use your plan book to guide your work this year, and as a reference next year. Document student behavior so that you can ask for help with special needs children, English language learners, and at-risk students.

Build a network of professional colleagues. Talk with other first-year teachers from your college experience, as they are probably going through the same things that you are. Take advantage of membership in a professional organization. Teachers should be members of a professional association in their discipline—math, reading, science, foreign languages, and the like, and also in a society for all teachers. Examples include Kappa Delta Pi (www.kdp.org), Phi Delta Kappa (www.pdkintl.org), and the Association for Middle Level Education (www.amle.org).

Read professional journals and attend professional development workshops and conferences. Do schools pay to send you to these events? A few school districts have money to send teachers to conferences, but often teachers must pay for these events themselves, and use sick or professional days to attend. Some districts do not even allow teachers to take the days to attend. The rules vary widely.

Take care of yourself during the first year of teaching. Know that it will be a busy, hectic year, with many nights and weekends spent planning. However, budget some time for friends, family, and personal time. New teachers report that they are exhausted by the end of the day and even more worn down by the end of each week. Many new teachers catch the colds and flu bugs that their students have. Teaching is not for the faint of heart! In the past, college professors admonished their new graduates not to get married or start families during the first two years of teaching. While no one should be that prescriptive about your personal life, know that it is difficult to juggle a new job and too many new responsibilities at once.

YOUR EVALUATIONS

The evaluation system of the school should be explained to you during new teacher orientation, or by an administrator or mentor early in the school year. Historically, teacher evaluations were based on a few classroom visits by an administrator. These visits were rarely announced, and teachers often felt that the administrator came to the classroom with a clipboard, seeming to "catch" the teacher doing anything wrong. This type of teacher evaluation has been called the "gotcha" approach, as the principal was looking for errors.

Evaluation systems have improved greatly, and many are guided by teacher contracts that are created in negotiations with the teachers' union or professional association and the local school board. Observations are still a major part of the annual evaluation and may be announced or unannounced. Expect at least three formal observations during your first year of teaching.

Student achievement is another means of evaluating teacher performance. In other words, your students' test scores may be evaluated as a factor in your annual evaluation. The higher the students' scores, the higher your evaluation. This is a much-debated issue, as some teachers work with more at-risk students than others. A teacher with many English language learners in the classroom may have lower standardized test scores than a teacher with no English language learners. What about students in high-poverty schools or ones with high student transiency? School districts may look at value-added test scores, not just the one standardized test score. This means that your students would be tested at the beginning of the year and again near the end of the year, and the growth in their scores is what would be measured. With this type of measurement, a second grade teacher whose students went from being nonreaders to reading at a first grade level would be considered as strong as a second grade teacher whose students went from second to third grade reading levels in that year.

Some school districts are looking at student and parent evaluations of teachers. We all remember the chance to evaluate our college professors in the end-of-course evaluation. This would now be done at middle and secondary schools. Some elementary schools would also use the system, having students as young as second and third grade evaluate their teachers. Parents would be sent evaluations for their input about the performance of their child's teachers.

It is also advised that you keep lots of documentation about your work. Consider keeping materials to make a portfolio of your first year of teaching. Include original activities, tests, and study guides that you have written. Keep a few samples of outstanding student work, with names removed. Take this portfolio with you to your end-of-year evaluation conference, and use it as your visual aid. If your contract is not renewed you will need a new portfolio to take with you to job interviews, so keep materials throughout the year. Update your resume as well, taking off some field experiences from college and adding complete information about your first year of teaching.

FAQS ABOUT THE FIRST YEAR OF TEACHING

1. Q: Is it true that the new hires get the worst students, the oldest materials, and the smallest classrooms? In other words, do the veterans get all the good students and good stuff?

   A: Many teachers would answer with a resounding "yes" to this question. However, most administrators would say that they strive to equalize assignments and resources. The truth lies somewhere in between. There is never an over-abundance of resources in today's schools, and someone has to have the small classroom and the old books. Often, a new hire is made at the last minute because of changing enrollments, and schools do scramble to equip a room. Remember that you work for a district, not an individual school, and that you may be assigned to any room, with a changing assignment at any time.

2. Q: Is it still possible to get tenure in today's schools, or is that a thing of the past?

   A: Earning tenure is not a thing of the past. Tenure laws are established by each state and do vary widely. Tenure is also called "right to fair dismissal" or "right to due process." In some states, having one's teaching contract renewed at the end of the third or even the second year of teaching means that the teacher has then received "tenure." In other states, or in certain districts, a teacher may have to apply for tenure when he/she reaches a certain amount of time in the district.

   You may still be fired after you are a tenured teacher. The difference is that the district must follow due process procedures for the nonrenewal of the contract. Before tenure, a teacher may be released at any time, and the district does not have to give a reason. Districts that lose student populations also have to release tenured teachers when schools are closed due to low enrollments. Be sure you understand the details of the tenure process in your new job.

3. Q: Should I join the teachers' union or professional association in my first year of teaching? If so, which one should I join and what are the advantages?

   A: The two major teachers' associations are the National Education Association (www.nea.org) and the American Federation of Teachers (www.aft.org). If you are not familiar with their services, read and find out about them. Generally, a local affiliate of one of these two associations represents the teachers in a district and bargains contracts and salaries for all teachers. Additionally, both organizations offer professional publications, conferences, and professional development opportunities. Membership rates vary, but may be several hundred dollars a year. If your district has "fair share" rules, and you don't join, you will still be charged a portion of the dues because you are being served by the association. Only you can decide, but only members have a vote, and local associations do vote on important issues such as contracts and salaries.

4. Q: Should I start work on my master's degree immediately after I get my first job? What are the advantages?

   A: There can be big advantages to earning a master's degree. First, you generally qualify for a significant pay raise, and second, you know more about your subject area and about teaching. The third reason to get a master's degree is to become more employable at a different level. Some people decide to earn a master's degree in administration/leadership, so that they might move into an administrative position in the future. A master's degree also allows you to consider a job at a community college, which may mean more money and a different teaching environment. However, going to college can be expensive, and the work for a master's degree is generally more difficult than undergraduate courses. You may want to wait a year or two until you are established. The best advice is to get your master's degree when you have the time and the opportunity.

5. Q: Can I get a master's degree online?

   A: Just as every college and university has a reputation, so too do the online programs. An online master's degree from a large, reputable university is quite different from an online master's from some other institutions. Before starting any master's program, find out its reputation and if your district accepts the degree for pay and advancement. Compare prices, too, as some online programs are much more expensive than traditional graduate programs at a college. Yes, you can get an online master's degree, and the acceptance of those degrees is improving, but not all programs are reputable ones. Do not be a teacher who pays $20,000 for an online degree and discovers that his/her district will not accept that institution's degrees. Look for accredited programs.

6. Q: What if I am not re-hired after my first year of teaching? Will that ruin my career?

    A: No, not being re-hired after the first year does not necessarily ruin a career. When the economy is down, schools must make budget cuts, and the first hired are the first released. Always be ready to explain a release due to a budget cut or school downsizing. When possible, ask for positive letters of recommendation from trusted colleagues and administrators. The first year is a learning experience.

THE STAGES OF A TEACHING CAREER

It can be argued that all the stages of a teaching career are meaningful. One begins as a new teacher, struggling to become established, but even those first challenging years can be exciting as you achieve success. After a few years in the profession, teachers progress into a stage of competence and mastery. Master teachers share their expertise with others by teaching workshops, serving as mentor teachers, and assuming leadership roles such as lead grade teacher or department chair. Many teachers choose to remain in the classroom, teaching full time, until retirement. Some teachers like the challenge of teaching, but change grade or discipline areas. Others choose to work in different areas of education.

Administration is a route for many teachers. They like working at the building level to run the school efficiently. If your interest lies in administration, you will need the advanced degree and appropriate certification for your state. In most cases, this is a master's degree in leadership. Some states seek administrators with specialist degrees, called EdS degrees, which are earned after 30 semester hours of work in addition to a master's degree. Talk to those working in administration for the specifics of how to move into a principal's position.

After a principalship, some choose to become superintendents, or to work in central administration, providing support to teachers through curriculum development, personnel, or other areas. Yes, these positions pay much more than teaching positions, but also generally require the employee to work a 12-month contract.

What else can one do with a teaching degree? Community colleges are a growth sector in education, as more and more students choose two-year programs for their value. Many community colleges seek master high school teachers with graduate degrees to teach on their campuses. Teaching loads vary, but often a community college instructor will teach four or five classes each semester, which means 12 to 15 contact hours a week with students. Of course, one can move into community college administration, as well. This may require a doctorate, but may not, depending on the position and the college's culture.

How does one move into teaching at a four-year college or university? These jobs do require a doctorate, especially if one seeks a full-time, tenure-track position. Elementary teachers may move into higher education to become teacher educators who train the next generation of elementary teachers. High school teachers may move into higher education to do the same, teaching undergraduates to be teachers, or they may choose to earn a doctorate in their discipline and then become a professor of math, science, Spanish, and the like.

The advantages of college teaching include flexibility and teaching nine to twelve hours a week, instead of five to six hours a day. However, research and publishing are a large part of college teaching. Earning tenure at any college or university usually depends upon one's ability to be a strong teacher and to publish on an annual basis. Jobs in higher education are increasingly competitive, and salaries are often similar to those in K–12 schools for professors of education.

Former teachers who move into higher education generally receive no credit for their experiences and start at the lowest rank and salary. For a veteran teacher with ten years of experience and a doctorate, this may actually mean a pay cut. It is not uncommon for K–12 teachers to retire as early as possible from their schools and then to take a part-time or adjunct position at a college or university. These jobs include some teaching and some supervision of teachers out in the field.

CLARIFYING YOUR GOALS

Even as you start your first teaching job, it can be a good idea to consider your options for the future. The advantages of teaching are many. Teaching remains the "family-friendly" profession, and while teaching and raising a family is far from easy, a teacher's schedule is much more compatible with child-rearing than other professions. You have the opportunity to stop out of teaching for a few years, and then return, which is unheard of in other professions. If you move, teachers are needed in all towns and cities all over the country.

Teachers from the United States are in demand around the world. Teachers of English are sought after in Asian countries and the opportunities for overseas teaching continue to increase. Some teachers choose a career in international schools and literally "teach their way around the world" through a variety of positions. These jobs generally require three to five years of experience and a master's degree.

Teaching can also be very challenging. Some reports indicate high drop-out rates of new teachers. Veteran teachers may actually encourage you to leave before you attain tenure, just because they are unhappy and trapped in their jobs. Avoid these teachers and seek a strong network of positive colleagues and friends.

No matter the venue you choose for your teaching, always consider yourself a professional. Work to raise student achievement and to raise the professional image of teaching. Being a life-long learner will help you to find fulfillment in teaching. Get your first job and keep growing.

Appendix

Thirty Secrets for Getting a Teaching Job

1. It takes a year to find a job. Start early.
2. A candidate should read at least two of the following books about getting a teaching job:

   American Association for Employment in Education. 2013. *Job Search Handbook for Educators*. www.aaee.org.

   Clement, M. C. 2007. *The Definitive Guide to Getting a Teaching Job*. Lanham, MD: Rowman & Littlefield.

   Kappa Delta Pi's *ABC's of Job-Hunting for Teachers* (2nd ed.).

   Pollock, R. 2011. *Teacher Interviews: How to Get Them and How to Get Hired*. Knoxville, TN: Advanta.

3. Visit at least three national web sites regularly. For example:

   www.schoolspring.com
   www.teachers-teachers.com
   www.k12jobspot.com

4. Visit your state's teacher job web site weekly.
5. Visit the web sites for individual districts regularly.
6. Create a template for a ONE-PAGE cover letter that will be modified for each use.
7. Create a one- to two-page resume that can be modified for each job.
8. A resume should be written in 11- or 12-point font, nothing smaller.

9. At least two people should read and edit your cover letter and resume before they are sent out.
10. Staff generally sort resumes first. So, make sure your certification stands out at the top.
11. Start your resume with a one- to two-line professional profile that makes you stand out.
12. Have a portfolio with only 6–8 key items (use a ½-inch binder).
13. Apply for jobs EXACTLY as the advertisement states.
14. Going in person to deliver paperwork is not recommended. See #13.
15. Calling or "stopping by" is not recommended.
16. Know how to answer a behavior-based question. These start with "tell about a time when . . . ," "how have you . . . ," "what has been your experience with . . ."
17. Use PAR and STAR to describe how you have dealt with a problem, an action taken, and the result (or situation, task, action, result).
18. Practice vignettes and answers to questions in front of a mirror and in front of other people.
19. Be ready to talk about curriculum, planning, classroom management, differentiation of instruction, assessment and grading, and parent communication.
20. Clean up you Facebook account and your voicemail message. If you use an electronic portfolio or web site, be aware of student confidentiality issues.
21. Attend job fairs up to a year in advance. Many are held in January, February, and March.
22. Use the services of your college career center. Many may offer credentials files as a way to send out letters of recommendation (online or on paper).
23. Buy a great career suit and use it.
24. Keep yourself looking professional—hair, nails, everything.
25. Carry only a small briefcase with your portfolio, extra resumes, and paper and pen to job fairs and interviews.
26. Know that telephone, online, and job fair interviews are used for screening. Do well at them and you will get an on-site interview.
27. Some on-site interviews now include a sample lesson to be taught.
28. Always be enthusiastic and energized. Your communication skills matter.
29. Send thank-you notes to interviewers.
30. Be aware of illegal and crazy questions.

Extra Credit: Know that you will hear conflicting advice. Read, study, and decide.

References

American Association for Employment in Education. (2013). *Job search handbook for educators*. Columbus, OH: author.

Anthony, R., and Coghill-Behrends, W. (2010). *Getting hired: A student teacher's guide to professionalism, resume development, and interviewing*. Dubuque, IA: Kendall-Hunt.

Campbell, D. M., Cignetti, P. B., Melenyzer, B. J., Nettles, D. H., and Wyman, R. M. (2011). *How to develop a professional portfolio: A manual for teachers* (5th ed.). Upper Saddle River, NJ: Pearson.

Canter, L. (2010). *Assertive discipline* (4th ed.). Bloomington, IN: Solution Tree.

Clement, M. C. (2010). *The ABC's of job-hunting for teachers* (2nd ed.). Indianapolis, IN: Kappa Delta Pi.

Clement, M. C. and Wilkins, E. A. (2011). *The induction connection: Facilitating new teacher success*. Indianapolis, IN: Kappa Delta Pi.

Costantino, P. M., De Lorenzo, M. N., and Tirrell-Corbin, C. (2008). *Developing a professional teaching portfolio: A guide to success* (3rd ed.). Upper Saddle River, NJ: Pearson.

Deems, R. S. (1994). *Interviewing: More than a gut feeling*. West Des Moines, IA: American Media Publishing.

Fitzwater, T. L. (2001). *Preparing for the behavior-based interview*. Boston: Thomson.

Janz, T., Hellervik, L., and Gilmore, D. C. (1986). *Behavior-description interviewing*. Upper Saddle River, NJ: Prentice-Hall.

Pollock, R. (2011). *Teacher interviews: How to get them and how to get hired*. Knoxville, TN: Advanta Press.

Wiseman, D. L., Knight, S. L., and Cooner, D. D., (2005). *Becoming a teacher in a field-based setting* (3rd ed.). Belmont, CA: Wadsworth.

Wong, H. K., and Wong, R. T. (2009). *The first days of school: How to be an effective teacher*. Mountain View, CA: Harry K. Wong Publications.

SPECIFIC WEB SITES

Salaries

www.teacherportal.com/teacher-salaries-by-state/
www.nassp.org/jobs/2010-principal-salary-survey
www.nea.org/home/38465.htm

Certification, State-by-State

www.education.uky.edu/AcadServ/content/50-states-certification-require-ments
www.teachers-teachers.com

Job trends

www.aaee.org

Teaching abroad

www.ciee.org
www.teachaway.com
www.uni.edu/placement/overseas/osfair.html

Interview portfolios

www.teachnet.com/how-to/employment/portfolios/index.html
www.best-job-interview.com/teacher-portfolio.html

Online recruitment sites

www.teachers-teachers.com
www.schoolspring.com
www.teaching-jobs.org

Index

About the Author

Mary C. Clement has researched the hiring of teachers for over twenty years, and her work has resulted in ten books and over a hundred articles. She has presented her work nationally to help candidates get their first teaching jobs, and has trained administrators in how to hire the best new teachers. A former high school teacher herself, she is a professor of teacher education at Berry College, north of Atlanta, Georgia. She earned her doctorate from the University of Illinois at Urbana–Champaign.